A CALL TO HOLINESS

Foreword by Paul Price

JOY HANEY

A CALL TO HOLINESS

Foreword by Paul Price

A Call to Holiness

by Joy Haney, B. Min.

Cover design by Kim Haney

Hazelwood, MO 63042-2299
Printing History: 2000, 2003, 2005, 2011

ISBN:978-1-56722-242-5
eISBN:978-1-56722-766-6

All Scripture quotations in this book are from the King James Version of the Bible unless otherwise identified.

Printed in United States of America

Printed by

WORD AFLAME PRESS
8855 Dunn Road, Hazelwood, MO 63042
www.pentecostalpublishing.com

Library of Congress Cataloging-in-Publication Data

Haney, Joy, 1942-
A call to holiness / Joy Haney.
p. cm.
Includes bibliographical references.
ISBN 1-56722-242-0
1. Holiness. I. Title.

BT767 .H28 1999
243—dc21 99-052284

CONTENTS

FOREWORD

"Holiness unto the Lord. Be ye holy for I am holy." Only God can explain who He is, and holiness must come by revelation of Jesus Christ, for He alone is holy. We are partakers of His holiness by our obedience to the exceedingly great and precious promises given to us in His Word. True holiness develops as we develop in the knowledge of our God and Savior Jesus Christ. Any outward application can be duplicated by a sinner, but no one can duplicate the nature of Jesus Christ. Our nature and our righteousness are as filthy rags and must be crucified before we can develop His righteousness and holiness in our everyday life.

As you can see, Sister Haney has opened a subject for which we are all striving to attain, and even though she is a good writer, there must first be a revelation of Jesus Christ before we can expect to have holiness unto the Lord. Truth is not received just by reading a book; there must first be an open heart and a desire to know truth in order to receive it.

The subject is deep and our understanding is limited, but we can benefit by allowing this book to open new light for all of us so that we can walk in true holiness. Of the many books written by Sister Haney, this is by far the greatest subject and greatest need today. Thank you, Sister Haney! We will join you in this great study.

Paul Price

PREFACE

As I read through my mother's book, I thought, This is wonderful—a message of holiness from a woman. Most of the time a man speaks or teaches women on holiness, but women have a way of talking to women that hits home. This book contains revelatory knowledge and wisdom on holiness. It will work wonders in opening the eyes of its readers. It will secure the foundation of any church.

Nathaniel Haney

ACKNOWLEDGMENTS

I give special thanks to the following people:

Kenneth Haney, my dear husband, who respects the appointment of the Lord in my life.

Angela, our daughter who is still at home. She helped me greatly during this time, cooking for my husband and taking care of the house.

Thanks to Kim Haney for all her hard work.

Margie McNall, who was supportive and very kind.

David Bernard, who took time out of his busy schedule to edit the book.

My mother, who has gone on to be with the Lord. I thank her for being a godly example of purity, righteousness, holiness, and kindness. She loved Jesus with all her heart. She loved the Bible and put that same love in my heart. I will always be grateful to her for teaching me how to pray with fervency and power!

My father, who is still a man of holiness and godliness. He is eighty-four years old, and is still on fire for God and looking for the soon return of the Lord Jesus Christ. He is a great man, for which I am thankful.

INTRODUCTION

In the past few months, I have received letters, e-mails, and personal requests from women who have asked me to speak out about what God wants for His people concerning His holiness.

On Monday, September 13, 1999, the Lord spoke to me and birthed within me a fire from heaven to write this book. I started Monday afternoon and worked nonstop until 11:00 that night. The following morning, Tuesday, I awakened at 3:30 A.M., prayed, and began to write, and once more worked nonstop until bedtime. It was as if I heard a voice in my head dictating to me. My fingers could not fly fast enough. It was like a river of inspiration flooding my mind and soul.

On Wednesday morning I began writing at 4:00 A.M., left the house for ladies prayer at 8:30 A.M., arrived back home at 12:00, and worked until 5:30 that evening. We were in a missions conference, so we went to church and were privileged to have the missionaries over to our house after service. I did not get to bed until 11:30 that night.

I awakened at 2:00 A.M. and worked nonstop until 11:00 that night. I began working Friday morning at 5:00 A.M. and just finished up at about 12:30 P.M.

It is an honor for God to choose me to write a book

on His holiness. The greater honor is that I felt His presence so close to me this week and know that I was just an emptied-out vessel that God chose to flow through to write this book.

It was an urgent call from heaven, and I laid everything aside and responded. My body was crying out at the exhausting schedule, but the unusual urgency and fire within me made it possible to respond to the Spirit. It is a miracle from heaven that this book came into being in the time that was allotted for it, but with God all things are possible to those who believe!

I will ever be grateful to my Lord and Master, Jesus Christ, who so tenderly deals with me and gives me insight through His precious Word. It is indeed an honor to write about His glory, holiness, and purity.

As the angels of the Lord cry continually around the throne, I join my voice with them and cry, "Worthy is the Lamb that was slain to receive power, and riches, and wisdom, and strength, and honour, and glory, and blessing" (Revelation 5:12).

May you open your heart to the Spirit and let Him speak to you through these pages. Remember, He wants His glory to rest upon you at all times. He desires for the world to see Him through you. You are His representative on earth, so represent Him well. "Now then we are ambassadors for Christ" (II Corinthians 5:20).

When you come to Christ, you are changed. "But we all, with open face beholding as in a glass the glory of the Lord, are changed into the same image from glory to glory, even as by the Spirit of the Lord" (II Corinthians 3:18).

Let His glory clothe you and shine through you, so that He may be glorified in the earth. Let there be no question to whom you belong.

In Earthen Vessels

The dear Lord's best interpreters
Are humble human souls;
The gospel of a life like His
Is more than books or scrolls.

From scheme and creed the light goes out;
The saintly fact survives,
The blessed Master none can doubt,
Revealed in holy lives.

—John Greenleaf Whittier

CHAPTER ONE

A Call to Holiness

A door opened and a man slipped quietly out into the dark streets of Boston. The streets were filled with red-coated British soldiers. There were sounds of shouted orders and the clank of muskets. In the confusion, none of the soldiers stopped the man, who walked with a dog at his heels. He made his way safely through town toward the waterfront to the house of his friend, Joshua.

"Joshua," he said when his friend greeted him at the door, "I need your help. The British soldiers are getting ready to attack. They're all over town already. I've warned our friends across the river to be ready, but I must get word to Sam Adams and John Hancock, who are hiding in Lexington."

Joshua whistled softly in surprise. "Paul," he said, "if Adams and Hancock are captured by the British, they will be sent back to England and hanged as traitors."

Paul replied, "That's right. You've got to row me across the river. I'll get a horse there and ride to Lexington to warn them."

"I'll row you across," said Joshua. "But we'd better hurry before the moon rises. There is a British ship blocking the river, and if they see us, we'll be done for."

When they were ready to go, Paul remembered that he did not have his spurs. He knew that he could not take the risk to go back through town and was in a quandary as to what to do, when he felt two little paws push against his knee. Suddenly Paul had an idea. The dog could run faster than a man could walk and could get past the soldiers with no trouble. He scribbled a note and tied it to his collar.

"Go straight home, Spot. Give the family this message. And come right back here with my spurs. Mind now! No stopping along the way."

By the time Joshua had the boat ready, Spot was back with the spurs. Paul untied the spurs and sent Spot back home to stay.

The small rowboat moved silently over the water. Paul and Joshua held their breath as the boat eased past the great black hull of the British ship. They reached the other side without being seen.

Minutes later, Paul was saddling a horse that had been given to him by one of his friends. He mounted the horse, waved goodbye, and was off.

Paul rode faster and faster as he and the small, strong

horse became used to each other. Each time he passed a farmhouse or a village he shouted the warning, "The Regulars are out! The British are coming!"

In these houses, muskets would be pulled from under mattresses, powder horns and shot pouches filled, and horses saddled in the barn. Soon there would be dozens, perhaps hundreds, of men on their way to Lexington.

Paul rode at full speed into the village of Medford. There were people to warn here. Paul raced through the town shouting to wake the people, "The Regulars are out! The British are coming!"

Without stopping, he left Medford and continued up the road. Now he was only a mile from the outskirts of Lexington. He would ride straight to the place where Adams and Hancock were hiding. He would warn them and go on to warn the people of Concord, when suddenly Paul saw two British officers, mounted and waiting in the shadow of an oak tree beside the road. He was so close he could see the pistols in their holsters.

They had already spotted him. One of the officers was turning his horse toward the oncoming rider. The other was starting the other way, to trap Paul if he escaped the first officer. Paul moved the reins across his horse's neck.

"Don't fail us now!" he whispered.

The horse turned without slowing, jumped a low stone fence, and raced out across the pasture on the other side. Paul bent low over its neck like an Indian, expecting at any moment to hear the sound of a pistol shot at his back.

Behind him the heavy British horses were getting off to a slow start. The first had just leaped the fence and was starting up the slope of the pasture. Paul spurred his horse up over the top of the rise and started down the other side. Ahead he could see a small woodland where he could lose the officers, if only he could reach it.

He had a hundred yards' start, but it was not enough for safety. He swerved his horse just in time to avoid a puddle of clay at the foot of the hill. The soft clay would have slowed him down enough for the British officers to catch up with him.

This was his chance to escape! If only the British soldiers wouldn't notice the puddle. As he rode toward the woods, he could hear the thunder of heavy hoofs back over his shoulder. A moment later the British horse was floundering in the clay puddle.

Minutes later Paul Revere was in Lexington, reining his horse in front of the place where Adams and Hancock were hiding. "Warn Adams and Hancock!" Paul shouted to the guards, "The Regulars are out! The British are coming!"

At once the guards rushed inside with the message, but Paul was gone already. He was riding toward Concord—riding to rouse the men who would, tomorrow morning, fire the shots that would be "heard around the world!"

Paul Revere's midnight ride on April 18, 1775, took place the night before the British attacked to start the Revolutionary War. But the Americans were prepared, thanks to Paul Revere.

This book is an urgent call to all Christians! It is midnight, and the Lord Jesus is coming back for a church without spot or wrinkle or any such thing. We can win the war against the enemy if we will awaken to the call of the Spirit. This book is a rousing call to true holiness.

II Timothy 1:9 gives that call: "Who hath saved us, and called us with an holy calling, not according to our works, but according to his own purpose and grace, which was given us in Christ Jesus before the world began."

Ephesians 5:27 states that His purpose is a clean church: "That he might present it to himself a glorious church, not having spot, or wrinkle, or any such thing; but that it should be holy and without blemish."

There it is. God wants a holy church!

We can only realize God's purpose through holiness. Hebrews 12:14 proclaims this truth: "Follow peace with all men, and holiness, without which no man shall see the Lord."

Holiness is the state or character of being holy. It is sanctity, saintliness, and consecration.

Before there can be holiness, there must first be a desire for holiness. A conscious act must follow desire. There must be an offering of self to the Lord and a compliance to the three W's: His will, His way, and His Word.

It is God's desire for His people to be holy. Leviticus 19:2 states, "Speak unto all the congregation of the children of Israel, and say unto them, Ye shall be holy: for I the LORD your God am holy."

Again in Leviticus 20:7 God told the Israelites, "Sanctify yourselves therefore, and be ye holy: for I am the LORD your God."

Sanctification means a state or quality of being sacred or holy; holiness of life and character; saintliness; godliness.

When people come into God's presence, there is always a feeling of lack on their part or of uncleanness. When Isaiah went into the Temple after King Uzziah died, he saw a vision of a holy God, sitting upon a throne, high and lifted up. His response was, "Woe is me! for I am undone; because I am a man of unclean lips, and I dwell in the midst of a people of unclean lips: for mine eyes have seen the King, the LORD of hosts" (Isaiah 6:5).

None of us can become holy by ourselves. We must have contact with the holy God in order to become filled with His holiness. Romans 15:16 states that we are "sanctified by the Holy Ghost." But it takes desire to receive the Holy Ghost.

It also requires an active response on the part of the person who desires to receive the Spirit and to be able to live in God's presence and hear His voice.

This truth is demonstrated in the story of Moses when he was on the backside of the desert. He came to the mountain in Horeb, and the angel of the Lord appeared unto him in a flame of fire coming out of a bush. The bush burned but it was not consumed.

"And Moses said, I will now turn aside, and see this great sight, why the bush is not burnt. And when the

Lord saw that he turned aside to see, God called unto him out of the midst of the bush and said, Moses, Moses. And he said, Here am I. And he said, Draw not nigh hither: put off thy shoes from off thy feet, for the place whereon thou standest is holy ground" (Exodus 3:3-5).

Notice, God did not call to Moses until Moses had first taken some action. He turned aside. He changed his direction. He stopped doing the normal things of life that he was accustomed to doing. He was getting ready to walk into the presence of a holy God.

God commanded Moses to take off his shoes. J. S. Exell explained the significance of this command:

> Put off thy shoes of sensuality, and other sins. Affections are the feet of the soul; keep them unclogged. The putting off of the sandals is a very ancient practice in worship. The rabbis say that the priests perform their service with bare feet, in token of purity and reverence.[1]

Matthew Henry gave further light on this action of Moses:

> Putting off the shoe was then what putting off the hat is now, a token of respect and submission. "The ground, for the present, is *holy ground*, made so by this special manifestation of the divine presence, during the continuance of which it must retain this character; therefore tread not

> on that ground with soiled shoes."[2]

Every spot where God appears to men and women is *holy ground*; therefore, everything must be laid aside in preparation for the great encounter of the Holy Spirit. God's presence is not to be treated lightly but with great respect.

The road to holiness is a journey of sacrifice mixed with love. It is the sacrifice of one's own ideas in exchange for truth. A love for God must lead the way. The journey must become an adventure. We must embark upon it with a right attitude. We must become a diligent seeker, filled with thankfulness for God's revelation, and keep an open heart to the ways of God, which are so foreign to the ways of humanity.

Holiness has always been and will always be. We cannot please God without holiness, and we cannot see Him without it. "Blessed are the pure in heart: for they shall see God" (Matthew 5:8).

Holiness was such an important requirement for the Israelites that God kept it ever before their eyes. Exodus 28:36 says, "And thou shalt make a plate of pure gold, and grave upon it, like the engravings of a signet, HOLINESS TO THE LORD." Verse 38 continues: "And it shall be upon Aaron's forehead, that Aaron may bear the iniquity of the holy things, which the children of Israel shall hallow in all their holy gifts; and it shall be always upon his forehead, that they may be accepted before the Lord."

To be holy means to be separated from sin and consecrated to God and His ideas. It is being separated from the world system and being in harmony with God. Throughout the Bible, God called men and women to sanctify themselves, that is, to cleanse themselves from all defilement, to forsake sin, and to come into harmony of life with God. The reason for God's demand upon men and women to be holy is that He wants them to be like Him. "Ye shall be holy: for I the LORD your God am holy" (Leviticus 19:2).

> Holiness (in the OT) is the perfect purity of God, which in and for itself excludes all fellowship with the world, and can only establish a relationship of free, electing love, whereby it asserts itself in the sanctification of God's people, their cleansing and redemption; therefore "the purity of God manifesting itself in atonement and redemption, and correspondingly in judgment."[3]

Christians in this generation do not have a sign before their eyes worn on the forehead of the minister. They have something better. They have God's Spirit inside them. This baptism of the Spirit can be experienced by "whosoever will" and was first poured out on the Day of Pentecost as recorded in Acts 2:1-4: "And when the day of Pentecost was fully come, they were all with one accord in one place. And suddenly there came a sound from heaven as of a rushing mighty wind, and it filled all the house where they were sitting. And there appeared unto them cloven tongues like as of fire, and it sat upon each of them. And they were all filled with the Holy Ghost, and began to speak with other tongues, as the Spirit gave them utterance."

Through this experience, humans beings became the temple of God. God chose to dwell in the bodies of men and women. It is the greatest privilege of humanity. God wants us to become holy and to allow Him to change us into becoming like Him. It is a lifetime experience of walking and talking with God, learning of Him, but it all begins with desire to know Him and to become like Him.

Ephesians 4:24 states that when we become a new person in Christ, we are created in holiness: "And that ye put on the new man, which after God is created in righteousness and true holiness."

> The term *holy* is constantly applied throughout NT to the divine Spirit. As proceeding from God, as the bearer of revelation, and as the mediator of spiritual life, the Spirit is pre-imminently holy. It is the special function of the Holy Spirit to make holy the souls of those in whom He dwells. This conception of the Spirit's nature and function is not prominent in OT, where the Spirit is scarcely more than a name for the power or presence of God. There He bestows strength upon heroes, skill upon artificers, and the knowledge of the divine will upon prophets. The designation of the Spirit as Holy accords entirely with the NT

> idea of the sanctifying function of the Spirit, and the hallowing of the people of God by inward consecration to Him. The Holy Spirit is conceived of as revealing the inner nature and essential goodness of God, and as accomplishing the transformation of men into His moral likeness.[4]

A wonderful aspect about the call to holiness is that we have Jesus Christ making intercession for us. Hebrews 7:25-26 states, "Wherefore he is able also to save them to the uttermost that come unto God by him, seeing he ever liveth to make intercession for them. For such an high priest became us, who is holy, harmless, undefiled, separate from sinners, and made higher than the heavens."

Romans 6:19 states that holiness should be a Christian's goal: "I speak after the manner of men because of the infirmity of your flesh: for as ye have yielded your members servants to uncleanness and to iniquity unto iniquity; even so now yield your members servants to righteousness unto holiness." Weymouth's translation says, "So you must now put them at the service of righteousness, with holiness as your goal."

II Corinthians 7:1 commands us to cleanse ourselves and aim at perfect holiness: "Having therefore these promises, dearly beloved, let us cleanse ourselves from all filthiness of the flesh and spirit, perfecting holiness in the fear of God." *The Twentieth Century New Testament* says, "And, in deepest reverence for God, aim at perfect holiness."

Romans 6:22 tells us, "But now being made free from

sin, and become servants to God, ye have your fruit unto holiness, and the end everlasting life." W. J. Coneybeare's translation says, "Your fruit is growth in holiness, and its end is life eternal."

A Christian, by faith and love, enters into fellowship with Christ and becomes conformed to Him and His ways. That is why Romans 12:1-2 says, "I beseech you therefore, brethren, by the mercies of God, that ye present your bodies a living sacrifice, holy, acceptable unto God, which is your reasonable service. And be not conformed to this world: but be ye transformed by the renewing of your mind, that ye may prove what is that good, and acceptable, and perfect, will of God."

Presenting a body is not just handing God a dead corpse. It is releasing to Him the body, mind, soul, and spirit. God demands that He owns us completely. In biblical times a sacrifice that was laid on top of the altar was not alive, it was dead. It had no will of its own. This is how God desires it to be in this generation. He wants to dwell in our bodies, control our minds, and cleanse our spirits. We should notice the words that apply to a Christian: "a living sacrifice," "holy," "acceptable to God," "not conformed to this world." Let us look closely at the definitions of these words listed below:

- *Living:* the state of one that lives; the fact of being or of continuing in life.

- *Sacrifice:* the act or process of making an offering to God; anything consecrated and offered to God; surrender of anything for the sake of something else; giving up of some desirable thing in behalf of a higher object.

- *Holy:* set apart to the service or worship of deity; hallowed; sacred.
- *Acceptable:* favorably received.
- *Conform:* to shape in accordance with; to be in accord or harmony; to comply or be obedient to or with.
- *World:* the customs, practices, and interests of men as social beings; manners and usages; the things of the world; temporal possessions.

What Romans 12 says is that if we are alive, we must consecrate and present our lives to God, being totally compliant to His Word and obedient to His commandments, and not shape ourselves according to the customs and ideas of the world.

A good example of this was demonstrated by an object lesson my daughter-in-law, Kim, once gave during a lesson at a Radiant Life Seminar. She spoke from Philippians 3:10: "That I may know him, and the power of his resurrection, and the fellowship of his sufferings, being made conformable unto his death."

She had her husband make her a small wooden cross and then as she held it up for the audience to see, she took tinfoil and began to mold it around the shape of the cross. This is what being conformable means: to shape oneself around the teachings of the Cross instead of around the world.

The preceding verse says, "And be found in him, not having mine own righteousness, which is of the law, but that which is through the faith of Jesus Christ, the righteousness which is of God by faith" (Philippians 3:9). The things people could not do by the law, they were able to do through the righteousness of Jesus Christ. Holiness is having the old man crucified and living in the power of His resurrection. It is letting the new nature of Jesus live in us and allowing His mind or His nature to control the fleshly nature.

"Let this mind be in you, which was also in Christ Jesus" (Philippians 2:5). What kind of mind does this verse refer to? It is a humble mind that is obedient to the will of God: "And being found in fashion as a man, he humbled himself, and became obedient unto death, even the death of the cross" (Philippians 2:8). God does not ask that we literally be crucified on a cross, but He asks us to crucify our own will and live in Christ: "I am crucified with Christ: nevertheless I live; yet not I, but Christ liveth in me: and the life which I now live in the flesh I live by the faith of the Son of God, who loved me, and gave himself for me" (Galatians 2:20).

Only when we stay dead to self can we let the world

see Jesus in us. When we come alive and demand our own fleshly or carnal way, then we begin to "stink" with the corruption of the flesh. "For he that soweth to his flesh shall of the flesh reap corruption; but he that soweth to the Spirit shall of the Spirit reap life everlasting" (Galatians 6:8). Our lower nature overrules the sweetness of His Spirit.

God's will is "that ye put off concerning the former conversation the old man, which is corrupt according to the deceitful lusts; and be renewed in the spirit of your mind; and that ye put on the new man, which after God is created in righteousness and true holiness" (Ephesians 4:22-24).

An unknown poet stated the principle well:

FILL US!

This the secret of the holy,
Not our holiness, but HIM.
Jesus! empty us and fill us
With Thy fullness to the brim.[5]

When Scripture says that God is holy, it refers to His purity, His perfection, and His goodness, and it thereby commands our fullest powers of adoration and reverence to Him.

Because of who He is, God deserves all reverence and honor. The song of Moses in Exodus 15:11 says, "Who is like unto thee, O LORD, among the gods? who is like thee, glorious in holiness, fearful in praises, doing wonders?" He is glorious in holiness! Many passages of Scripture describe the holiness of God, as we see by the following points.

God's Throne Is Called Holiness

"God reigneth over the heathen: God sitteth upon the throne of his holiness" (Psalm 47:8).

Holiness Becomes His House

"Thy testimonies are very sure: holiness becometh thine house, O Lord, for ever" (Psalm 93:5).

His Courts Are Called Holiness

"But they that have gathered it shall eat it, and praise the Lord; and they that have brought it together shall drink it in the courts of my holiness" (Isaiah 62:9).

His Habitation Is Called Holiness

"Look down from heaven, and behold from the habitation of thy holiness and of thy glory" (Isaiah 63:15).

Holiness Is Beautiful

"Thy people shall be willing in the day of thy power, in the beauties of holiness from the womb of the morning" (Psalm 110:3).

God Has a Highway of Holiness

"And an highway shall be there, and a way, and it

shall be called The way of holiness; the unclean shall not pass over it" (Isaiah 35:8).

There Is a Spirit of Holiness

"And declared to be the Son of God with power, according to the spirit of holiness, by the resurrection from the dead" (Romans 1:4).

May you be filled with that spirit of holiness. May it burn within you like a mighty fire. May you become passionate about God and His ways, following after Him with a pure heart, for only the pure in heart shall see God.

Living a holy life will be worth it, for at the end of time God will weigh every person on a scale. One side will be *righteous and holy,* and the other side will be *unjust and filthy*. Everything boils down to these two categories according to Revelation 22:11-12, which says, "He that is unjust, let him be unjust still: and he which is filthy, let him be filthy still: and he that is righteous, let him be righteous still: and he that is holy, let him be holy still. And, behold, I come quickly; and my reward is with me, to give every man according as his work shall be."

What do these four words represent? Let us note the following definitions:

- *Righteous*: godly, blameless, upright, just, free from sin.

- *Holy*: spiritually whole, free from sinful affectations, pure in heart.

- *Unjust*: dishonest, faithless, wrongful, iniquitous.

- *Filthy*: defiled with filth, whether material or moral; disgustingly dirty; foul, obscene, impure.

Proverbs 16:2 states, "All the ways of a man are clean in his own eyes; but the Lord weigheth the spirits."

God's Eternal Scale

I Thessalonians 4:7 states God's purpose for His children in a nutshell: "For God hath not called us unto uncleanness, but unto holiness."

As you read this book may you feel the urgent call to

God's holiness and serve the Lord in holiness as prophesied by Zacharias at the birth of John the Baptist: "That he would grant unto us, that we being delivered out of the hand of our enemies might serve him without fear, in holiness and righteousness before him, all the days of our life" (Luke 1:74-75).

She Walks in Beauty

She walks in beauty, like the night
Of cloudless climes and starry skies;
And all that's best of dark and bright
Meet in her aspect and her eyes:
Thus mellowed to that tender light
Which heaven to gaudy day denies.

One shade the more, one ray the less,
Had half impaired the nameless grace
Which waves in every raven tress,
Or softly lightens o'er her face;
Where thoughts serenely express
How pure, how dear their dwelling place.

And so on that cheek, and o'er that brow,
So soft, so calm, yet eloquent,
The smiles that win, the tints that glow,
But tell of days in goodness spent,
A mind at peace with all below,
A heart whose love is innocent!

—Lord Byron

CHAPTER TWO

Holy in Heart

"The pure in heart shall see God." There is power in purity. One of the knights of King Arthur's Round Table was Sir Galahad, called the Maiden Knight because of his pure life. Tennyson depicted him as saying, "My strength is as the strength of ten, because my heart is pure."

There is power in purity. When the Holy Spirit comes upon a person to cleanse his heart, He also brings power—power to resist temptation, to stand up and be counted, to do the right thing every time.

Such purity was found in the parents of John the Baptist. They were two people, a priest named Zacharias and his wife, Elisabeth, who desired a child. "And they were both righteous before God, walking in all the commandments and ordinances of the Lord blameless" (Luke 1:6).

One day while Zacharias was doing his priestly duties, an angel appeared unto him. Zacharias became afraid, but the angel said, "Fear not, Zacharias: for thy prayer is heard; and thy wife Elisabeth shall bear thee a son, and thou shalt call his name John" (Luke 1:13).

The next thing the angel told Zacharias about John the Baptist, as he became known, was this: "He shall be filled with the Holy Ghost, even from his mother's womb" (Luke 1:15).

The holiness of God was in John's heart, so that all who heard him speak sensed it. Even King Herod was affected by John. "For Herod feared John, knowing that he was a just man and an holy, and observed him; and when he heard him, he did many things, and heard him gladly" (Mark 6:20).

People will know if we have holiness in our heart. We do not have to tell them. Our actions, speech, demeanor, and attitude will advertise our heart condition. It is important to seek the Lord and follow after His holiness.

David instructed the princes to seek the Lord and build a Temple for His holy vessels: "Now set your heart and your soul to seek the LORD your God; arise therefore, and build ye the sanctuary of the LORD God, to bring the ark of the covenant of the LORD, and the holy vessels of God, into the house that is to be built to the name of the LORD" (I Chronicles 22:19). Just as God wanted holy vessels in the Temple under the rule of David and Solomon, so today He wants holy vessels, that is, holy people.

We can either be sanctified, honorable vessels or dishonorable vessels. "But in a great house there are not only vessels of gold and of silver, but also of wood and of earth; and some to honour, and some to dishonour. If a man therefore purge himself from these, he shall be a vessel unto honour, sanctified, and meet for the master's use, and prepared unto every good work" (II Timothy 2:20-21).

Not only are God's children likened to vessels, but they are also likened to a temple. I Corinthians 3:16-17 states emphatically: "Know ye not that ye are the temple of God, and that the Spirit of God dwelleth in you? If any man defile the temple of God, him shall God destroy; for the temple of God is holy, which temple ye are."

What does it mean to defile? Why would God destroy someone who defiles His temple? Let us note the following definitions of *defile* in *Webster's Dictionary*.

- To make filthy or unclean.
- To corrupt the purity or perfection of; to debase.
- To pollute.
- To rob of chastity; to ravish; to violate.

Holiness and cleanness are practically identical. David said in Psalm 51:10-11: "Create in me a clean heart, O God; and renew a right spirit within me. Cast me not away from thy presence; and take not thy holy spirit from me."

It is good to be aware of the difference between clean and unclean. Leviticus 10:10 gives God's admonition not to not turn a deaf ear to the problem, or pretend we do not see it, but to draw the line: "That ye may put difference between holy and unholy, and between unclean and clean."

There is a danger in not making a difference between the holy and the unholy: "Her priests have violated my law, and have profaned mine holy things: they have put no difference between the holy and the profane, neither have they shewed difference between the unclean and the clean, and have hid their eyes from my sabbaths, and I am profaned among them." (Ezekiel 22:26).

The Lord further stated that He looked for a man to stand in the gap, show his people the difference, and help them clean up the mess, but He could find no one. What happened? Ezekiel 22:31 gives the terrible details: "Therefore have I poured out mine indignation upon them; I have consumed them with the fire of my wrath: their own way have I recompensed upon their heads, saith the Lord GOD."

Recompense means to give an equivalent for or return in kind. God's judgment is still the same, as we see in Galatians 6:7-8: "Be not deceived; God is not mocked: for whatsoever a man soweth, that shall he also reap. For he that soweth to his flesh shall of the flesh reap corruption; but he that soweth to the Spirit shall of the Spirit reap life everlasting."

The important thing is to have the understanding of what is holy and what is unholy. Many people are confused about what is holy these days. Proverbs 9:10 states, "The fear of the LORD is the beginning of wisdom: and the knowledge of the holy is understanding." If we want to have a spirit of understanding and eradicate all confusion, we must study the Bible and learn to know the holy God.

Romans 8:6-8 says, "For to be carnally minded is death; but to be spiritually minded is life and peace. Because the carnal mind is enmity against God: for it is not subject to the law of God, neither indeed can be. So then they that are in the flesh cannot please God."

It is imperative for the Christian to keep his mind pure and in tune with God. If not, the result is sure death. Henry Ward Beecher described that death:

> Now, take a man that is spiritually dead. Pinch his conscience; he does not start. Bring before him the law, and let it thunder in his ears; it makes no impression upon him. Pierce him with the sword of the Spirit; he does not feel it; he is not susceptible to fear; he has no moral sensibility. And you say that that man is spiritually dead because he is not alive to Divine influences.[6]

To be holy in heart and alive to God should be the number-one desire of every Christian. To be called a man or woman with a pure heart after God is the greatest thing that anyone could say about us.

We see this test of character in Acts 6, when a complaint arose that the Grecian widows were being neglected. The apostles called the disciples together and told them to choose "seven men of honest report, full of the Holy Ghost and wisdom, whom we may appoint over this business. But we will give ourselves continually to prayer, and to the ministry of the word" (Acts 6:3-4).

This decision pleased the multitude, and they selected seven, including "Stephen, a man full of faith and of the Holy Ghost" (Acts 6:5).

Significantly, it was not merely the spirit of the men that made them honest and of good report; it was the Holy Ghost. God is holy, and He dwelt within them. His holiness controlled their actions, so that there was no room for sin to rule.

John Wesley's mother taught her children the following about sin: "Would you judge the lawfulness of a pleasure? Take this rule: Whatever weakens your reason, impairs the tenderness of your conscience, obscures your vision of God, or takes away the relish of spiritual things or increases the authority of your body over your mind, that is sin."[7]

It is imperative to respect the Spirit of God, which He has allowed to dwell inside the heart of humanity. It is God who makes men and women holy. Because He is holy, they are holy. Romans 11:16 expresses a principle that we can apply here: "For if the firstfruit be holy, the lump is also holy: and if the root be holy, so are the branches."

Jesus spoke about the vine and the branches in John 15. "I am the vine, ye are the branches: He that abideth in me, and I in him, the same bringeth forth much fruit: for without me ye can do nothing" (John 15:5).

God knows who is connected to the vine, for "the LORD looketh on the heart" (I Samuel 16:7). Since God sees the heart, it is imperative to guard and protect the condition of the spiritual heart. Let us note the following important points about the heart.

All of Life Flows from the Heart

"Keep thy heart with all diligence; for out of it are the issues of life" (Proverbs 4:23).

The Heart Is Naturally Deceitful; There Must Be a Heart Change

"The heart is deceitful above all things, and desperately wicked: who can know it? I the LORD search the heart, I try the reins, even to give every man according to his ways, and according to the fruit of his doings" (Jeremiah 17:9-10).

"And I will give them an heart to know me, that I am the LORD: and they shall be my people, and I will be their God: for they shall return unto me with their whole heart" (Jeremiah 24:7).

"But those things which proceed out of the mouth come forth from the heart; and they defile the man. For out of the heart proceed evil thoughts, murders, adulteries, fornications, thefts, false witness, blasphemies" (Matthew 15:18-19).

The following story shows how Christ can change a heart. It is told by a student of a chemistry class:

> In the chemistry class we learned how acids act on different substances. In the course of our experiment the professor gave us a bit of gold and told us to dissolve it. We left it all night in the strongest acid we had and tried combinations of acids, then finally told him we thought gold could not be dissolved. He smiled, "I knew you could not dissolve gold," he said; "none of the acids you have there will attack it; but try this," and he handed us a bottle labeled "Nitromuriatic Acid (Aqua Regia)."
>
> We poured some of its contents into the tube that held the piece of gold; and the gold that had resisted so easily all the other acids quickly disappeared in the "royal water." The gold at last had found its master. The next day in the classroom the professor asked, "Do you know why it is called Royal Water?"
>
> "Yes," we replied, "it is because it is the master of gold, which can resist almost anything else that can be poured on it."
>
> Then he said, "Boys, it will not hurt the lesson today if I take time to tell you that there is one

other substance that is just as impervious as gold; it cannot be touched or changed, though a hundred attempts are made upon it. That substance is the sinful heart. Trial and affliction, riches and honor, imprisonment and punishment will not soften or master it. Education and culture will not dissolve and purify it. There is but one element that has power over it—the blood of Jesus Christ the Saviour, the aqua regia of the soul."[8]

It Is Important to Prepare the Heart to Seek the Lord

"And he did evil, because he prepared not his heart to seek the LORD" (II Chronicles 12:14).

"But Hezekiah prayed for them, saying, The good LORD pardon every one that prepareth his heart to seek God. . . . And the LORD hearkened to Hezekiah, and healed the people" (II Chronicles 30:18-20).

"For Ezra had prepared his heart to seek the law of the LORD, and to do it, and to teach in Israel statutes and judgments" (Ezra 7:10).

It Is Important to Get the Word of God in the Heart

"The mouth of the righteous speaketh wisdom, and his tongue talketh of judgment. The law of his God is in his heart; none of his steps shall slide" (Psalm 37:30-31).

"Thy word have I hid in mine heart, that I might not sin against thee" (Psalm 119:11).

"Let not mercy and truth forsake thee: bind them about thy neck; write them upon the table of thine heart:

so shalt thou find favour and good understanding in the sight of God and man" (Proverbs 3:3-4).

God Wants to Fill Our Heart and Being

"That he would grant you, according to the riches of his glory, to be strengthened with might by his Spirit in the inner man; that Christ may dwell in your hearts by faith; that ye, being rooted and grounded in love, may be able to comprehend with all saints what is the breadth, and length, and depth, and height; and to know the love of Christ, which passeth knowledge, that ye might be filled with all the fulness of God" (Ephesians 3:16-19).

> Katherine Bevis tells how among the students at a well-known college there was a young man who had to get about on crutches. He had an unusual talent for friendliness and optimism and so won the deep respect of his classmates. One day a student asked him what had caused his deformity. "Infantile paralysis," he replied briefly, not wishing to elaborate on his difficulties. "With a misfortune like that, how can you face the world so?" inquired his classmate. "Oh," replied the young Christian, smiling, "the disease never touched my heart."[9]

The disease that so often touches the heart is pride. Pride was the reason for Lucifer's fall from heaven. Pride will always separate man from God.

Proud Hearts Are an Abomination to God

"Every one that is proud in heart is an abomination to the LORD: though hand join in hand, he shall not be unpunished" (Proverbs 16:5).

"Every way of a man is right in his own eyes: but the LORD pondereth the hearts. To do justice and judgment is more acceptable to the LORD than sacrifice. An high look, and a proud heart, and the plowing of the wicked, is sin" (Proverbs 21:2-4).

Oh! Why should the spirit of mortal be proud?
Like a swift-fleeting meteor, a fast-flying cloud,
A flash of the lightning, a break of the wave,
Man passeth from life to his rest in the grave.

The leaves of the oak and the willow shall fade,
Be scattered around, and together be laid;
And the young and the old, and the low and the high
Shall molder to dust and together shall die.

'Tis the wink of an eye, 'tis the draught of a breath,
From the blossom of health to the paleness of death,
From the gilded saloon to the bier and the shroud—
Oh! Why should the spirit of mortal be proud?

—William Knox

Consecration of Self

True conversion to God involves the consecration of ourselves and of all that we have to Him, so far as we understand what is implied in this. But, at first, converts are by no means aware of all that is involved in the highest forms of consecration. To gain such knowledge is a work of time; and growth in the favor of God is conditioned on making a full surrender and consecration to God of everything we are, and have, and desire, and love, as fast as these objects are presented to thought.

—Charles G. Finney

CHAPTER THREE

Holy in Separation

God wanted His people in the Old Testament to be separated so that the glory of His power could be demonstrated through them. The separation from the heathen nations was their distinct mark of power with God. He chose them to be His children, and as long as they worshipped Him only, He did great and mighty things for them. When they went after other gods, His judgment replaced the glory!

The Book of Ezra gives a dark picture of a people who disobeyed the commandment God gave to them to be separated. The princes went to Ezra and said, "The people of Israel, and the priests, and the Levites, have not separated themselves from the people of the lands, doing according to their abominations, . . . for they have taken of their daughters for themselves, and for their sons: so that the holy seed have mingled themselves with the people of those lands" (Ezra 9:1-2).

This caused great distress to Ezra and he rent his garment, pulled his hair out and sat down in astonishment. He then fell on his knees and spread out his hands unto the Lord God and cried, "O my God, I am ashamed and blush to lift up my face to thee, my God: for our iniquities are increased over our head, and our trespass is grown up unto the heavens" (Ezra 9:6).

The two words that emerge strong and clear are *mingle* and *separate*. They are antonyms, meaning that they are the opposite of each other. Let us note their definitions from *Webster's Dictionary*.

Mingle

- To combine or join one thing with another.
- To unite or join in company.
- To make or mix by mixing the ingredients of.
- To confuse or confound.

When there is a mingling and mixing together between a child of God and the ways of the world, the result is always confusion. Clarity of thought is gone, as well as good judgment. This causes the one who mingles with the world to lose his or her identity and relationship with Christ.

Separate

- Unconnected; not united or associated; distinct.
- Divided from another or others; severed.
- Being apart from others.
- Not common or shared; peculiar.

Webster's Dictionary defines the word *peculiar* as follows:

- Belonging especially or exclusively to an individual, as property or possessions. Characteristic of or belonging to one only.
- Separate; distinct. Different from the usual or normal.
- Unusual; an exclusive property or privilege.

We belong to God and are His exclusive property. He purchased us with His blood. It is a privilege to be His child.

It is very important that we not become defensive because of our peculiarity when people stare at us or ask why we are different. It is very important to let the people who ask us a question, feel a river of love flowing from us to them. We are not different just to be different but to make a difference in the lives of others for Christ!

I Peter 2:9 instructs Christians to be different, separate, distinct, belonging only to Christ: "But ye are a chosen generation, a royal priesthood, an holy nation, a peculiar people; that ye should shew forth the praises of him who hath called you out of darkness into his marvellous light." I Peter 2:11 further implores us to stay away from fleshly lusts: "Dearly beloved, I beseech you as strangers and pilgrims, abstain from fleshly lusts, which war against the soul." *Webster's Dictionary* defines *stranger* and *pilgrim* as follows:

Stranger

- One who is strange. One who comes from a foreign land. [In this case, a Christian's citizenship is in heaven, not in the world.]

- A person who is unknown or with whom one is unacquainted. One ignorant of, or unfamiliar with, a specified object. [The world. The less we become acquainted with the world, the better off we and our family will be.]

Pilgrim

- One who journeys in alien lands.

- One who travels, usually far, and often in strange lands.

Some of God's people have become too acquainted with the world and its ways. There is not a definite line drawn, so as to make a distinction. They have gotten too close to the world.

Many years ago a woman of wealth wanted to hire a coachman. Three persons applied for the job. When she spoke to the applicants, she asked each the same question: "Tell me, if you drove my coach around a steep corner with a precipice on one side, how near could you go to the precipice?" The first applicant said, "I think I could keep within twelve inches of the precipice and we would be perfectly safe!" The next man said, "I could take you a hair's breadth and we would still be safe!" The third man said, "Madam, if I'm going to get this job and you want me as your coachman, I'm telling you that when we go around that corner, I'm keeping as far from that precipice as I can!" He was the one employed.

Too many Christians are on a precipice trying to get as close to the world as possible while staying in the church, and they are a hair's breadth away from falling headlong to destruction. It is best to keep as far from the world as possible.

The New Testament commands the church to be separate from and love not the world and her evil ways. I John 2:15-17 says, "Love not the world, neither the things that are in the world. If any man love the world, the love of the Father is not in him. For all that is in the world, the lust of the flesh, and the lust of the eyes, and the pride of life, is not of the Father, but is of the world. And the world passeth away, and the lust thereof: but he that doeth the will of God abideth for ever."

Dr. V. Raymond Edman described the world as follows: "The *world* is a spirit, and is expressed in things. It defies exact definition because it is a spirit. The closest working definition I have found is that of John Wesley: 'Whatever cools my affection toward Christ is the world.'"[10]

The will of God is for us not to love the world or anything in it. It is all about *choice*. All of us will decide what we will be associated with and to whom we will belong. Each system has an identity attached to it. We will either be identified with God or the world. The two cannot mix or mingle.

II Corinthians 6:17 commands, "Wherefore come out from among them, and be ye separate, saith the Lord, and touch not the unclean thing; and I will receive you." For God to receive us, there must be separation from what is unclean.

The preceding verses clearly describe this separation: "Be ye not unequally yoked together with unbelievers: for what fellowship hath righteousness with unrighteousness? and what communion hath light with darkness? and what concord hath Christ with Belial? or what part hath he that believeth with an infidel? and what agreement hath the temple of God with idols? for ye are the temple of the living God; as God hath said, I will dwell in them, and walk in them; and I will be their God, and they shall be my people" (II Corinthians 6:14-16).

Dr. Wilbur Chapman had what he called "My Rule for Christian Living." He said, "The rule that governs my life is this: anything that dims my vision of Christ, or takes away my taste for Bible study, or cramps my prayer life, or makes Christian work difficult is wrong for me, I must, as a Christian, turn away from it."

This is a good rule of thumb for all to follow! There must be a distinct line of separation. There is too much gray area and too much tolerance for sin in this generation! People find it hard to blush at things they once had a strong aversion to and made a public outcry against. They are becoming desensitized to sin.

"Christians should avoid all appearance of evil instead of doing a balancing act on the line of demarcation between good and evil: 'Abstain from all appearance of evil' (I Thessalonians 5:22)."[11]

Many things have caused the demise of holiness in the lives of some Christians and caused America's morals to decay, but one of those things is television. Several years ago, Billy Graham, a respected minister around the world, was quoted as saying: "I think television is having a detrimental effect on Christians. They are no longer sensitive to sin! Television has brought the nightclub into the home along with violence and sex, things which Christians looked upon ten years ago with abhorrence. They are gradually becoming desensitized, and I can cite case after case where Christians now watch these things on television without feeling any twinge of conscience."[12]

I received the following reading in my e-mail recently, which is good food for thought:

THE STRANGER

A few months before I was born, my dad met a stranger who was new to our small town. From the beginning, Dad was fascinated with this enchanting newcomer and soon invited him to live with our family. The stranger was quickly accepted and was around to welcome me into the world a few months later.

As I grew up I never questioned his place in our family. Mom taught me to love the Word of God, and Dad taught me to obey it. But the stranger was our storyteller. He could weave the most fascinating tales. Adventures, mysteries, and comedies were daily conversations. He could hold our whole family spellbound for hours each evening. He was like a friend to the whole family. He took Dad, Bill, and me to our first major league baseball game. He was always encouraging us to see the movies, and he even made arrangements to introduce us to several movie stars.

The stranger was an incessant talker. Dad didn't seem to mind, but sometimes Mom would quietly get up, while the rest of us were enthralled with one of his stories of faraway places, and go to her room, where she would read the Bible and pray. I wonder now if she ever prayed that the stranger would leave.

You see, my Dad ruled our household with certain moral convictions. But this stranger never felt an obligation to honor them. Profanity, for example, was not allowed in our house—not from us, from our friends, or adults. Our longtime visitor, however, used occasional four-letter words that burned my ears and made Dad squirm. To my knowledge the stranger was never confronted. My Dad was a teetotaler who didn't permit alcohol in his home, not even for cooking. But the stranger felt like we needed exposure and enlightened us to other ways of life. He offered us beer and other alcoholic beverages often. He made cigarettes look tasty, cigars manly, and pipes distinguished.

He talked freely (too much, too freely) about sex. His comments were sometimes blatant, sometimes suggestive, and generally embarrassing. I know now that my early concepts of the man/woman relationship were influenced by the stranger.

As I look back, I believe it was the grace of God and my mother's prayers that the stranger did not influence us more. Time after time he opposed the values of my parents, yet he was seldom rebuked and never asked to leave.

More than thirty years have passed since the stranger moved in with the young family on Morningside Drive. But if I were to walk into my parents' den today, you could still see him sitting over in a corner, waiting for someone to listen to him talk and watch him draw his pictures. His name? We always just called him by his initials . . . TV.

Twenty years ago in Falls Church, Virginia, PTA members kept eyes fixed on TV programs through the hours children would be viewing them. They observed 185 programs for 114 ½ hours, saw 281 assaults, 117 killings, 19 robberies, 16 kidnappings, 10 murder conspiracies, 3 arsons, 3 extortions, 3 jailbreaks, 1 lynching, 1 bombing, and 1 suicide. I wonder what it would be today?

The core of the matter is choice. There are two systems or two worlds: God's and the present world system. Every day we make choices as to which world we will live in. Each world has its own set of laws, customs, traditions, and ways. We cannot mix them. They are totally different from each one. We decide who or what will influence us. We decide what we look at, what we read, where we go, whom we associate with, what we partake of, and who will be our master.

There is a continual war within the heart of each individual, as Ephesians 6:12 describes: "For we wrestle not against flesh and blood, but against principalities, against powers, against the rulers of the darkness of this world, against spiritual wickedness in high places."

God has allowed Satan to have limited power for a limited time. Satan walks to and fro throughout the earth trying to deceive people into following his evil plans. The day will come when he will be chained, thrown into the bottomless pit, and cast forever into the lake of fire. Until that time comes, he attempts to pull us down with him.

Christians must remember that they are citizens from another country and that their king is Jesus. He sits upon the throne as described in Revelation 4:2-3, 5: "And immediately I was in the spirit: and, behold, a throne was set in heaven, and one sat on the throne. And he that sat was to look upon like a jasper and a sardine stone: and there was a rainbow round about the throne, in sight like unto an emerald. . . . And out of the throne proceeded lightnings and thunderings and voices: and there were lamps of fire burning before the throne."

The story is told of the Spaniards who were besieging the little town of St. Quentin, on the frontiers of France. Its ramparts were in ruins; fever and famine were decimating its defenders; treason existed among its terrified population. One day the Spaniards shot over the walls a shower of arrows, to which were attached little slips of parchment, promising the inhabitants that if they would surrender, their lives and property would be spared.

The governor of the town was the great leader of the Huguenots, Gaspard de Coligni. As his sole answer he took a piece of parchment, tied it to a javelin, wrote on it the two words *Regem habemus*—"We have a king!"—and hurled it back into the camp of the enemy. There was his one answer to all their threats and all their inducements.

When the enemy of our soul keeps badgering us,

threatening us, and tempting us to give in, we can simply hurl back at him, "I have a King!" Romans 8:31 states, "What shall we then say to these things? If God be for us, who can be against us?"

The question is, "Who is King of your life?" Can you always say, with a sincere heart, in every situation, "What would Jesus do?" and then do accordingly?

You can choose to overcome and keep a pure heart before God, but it must be a daily vigil. This is done through prayer, reading of the Word, resisting Satan, and being aware of his devices, as the following Scripture verses indicate:

"Praying always with all prayer and supplication in the Spirit" (Ephesians 6:18). This verse comes at the end of the discourse on the armor a Christian is to be covered with.

"Neither give place to the devil" (Ephesians 4:27). Do not give an ear to his voice. Speak the Word back to his temptations, or send Jesus to the door when he knocks.

Martin Luther was asked one time how he overcame the devil. He replied:

> Well, when he comes knocking upon the door of my heart, and asks, "Who lives here?" the dear Lord Jesus goes to the door and says, "Martin Luther used to live here but he has moved out. Now I live here." The devil seeing the nail-prints in the hands, and the pierced side, takes flight immediately.

"Be sober, be vigilant [aware]; because your adversary the devil, as a roaring lion, walketh about, seeking whom he may devour: whom resist stedfast in the faith" (I Peter 5:8-9).

"Submit yourselves therefore to God. Resist the devil, and he will flee from you" (James 4:7).

"Ye are of God, little children, and have overcome them: because greater is he that is in you, than he that is in the world" (I John 4:4). In Christ, we have more power than the devil!

"For the word of God is quick, and powerful, and sharper than any two edged sword, piercing even to the dividing asunder of soul and spirit, and of the joints and marrow, and is a discerner of the thoughts and intents of the heart" (Hebrews 4:12). The Word will cut away the devil's thoughts and evil temptations.

It would be a good thing if all believers would adopt for their own life the following consecrations of Jonathan Edwards, a preacher known for his famous message "Sinners in the Hands of an Angry God," preached in the 1700s:

> I claim no right to myself—no right to this understanding, this will, these affections that are in me; neither do I have any right to this body or its members—no right to this tongue, to these hands, feet, ears, or eyes.
>
> I have given myself clear away and not retained anything of my own. I have been to God

this morning and told Him I have given myself wholly to Him. I have given every power, so that for the future I claim no right to myself in any respect. I have expressly promised Him, for by His grace I will not fail. I take Him as my whole portion and felicity, looking upon nothing else as any part of my happiness. His law is the constant rule of my obedience.

I will fight with all my might against the world, the flesh, and the devil to the end of my life. I will adhere to the faith of the Gospel, however hazardous and difficult the profession and practice of it may be.

I receive the blessed Spirit as my Teacher, Sanctifier, and only Comforter, and cherish all admonitions to enlighten, purify, confirm, comfort, and assist me. This I have done.

I pray God, for the sake of others, to look upon this as a self-dedication, and receive me as His own. Henceforth, I am not to act in any respect as my own. I shall act as my own if I ever make use of any of my powers to do anything that is not to the glory of God, or to fail to make the glorifying of Him my whole and entire business.

If I murmur in the least at afflictions; if I am in any way uncharitable; if I revenge my own case; if I do anything purely to please myself, or omit anything because it is a great denial; if I trust to myself; if I take any praise for any good which

Christ does by me; or if I am in any way proud, I shall act as my own and not God's. I purpose to be absolutely His.[13]

Sermons We See

I'd rather see a sermon than
hear one, any day;
I'd rather one would walk with
me than merely tell the way;
The eye's a better pupil and
more willing than the ear.
Fine counsel is confusing,
but example's always clear,
And the best of all the preachers
are the men who live their creeds,
For to see good put in action
is what everybody needs.

I soon can learn to do it if
you'll let me see it done;
I can watch your hand in actions,
but your tongue too fast may run.
And the lecture you deliver may
be very wise and true,
But I'd rather get my lessons

by observing what you do.
For I might misunderstand you
and the high advice you give.
But there's no misunderstanding
how you act and how you live.

—Edgar Guest

CHAPTER FOUR

HOLY IN SPIRIT AND ATTITUDES

A spirit exudes forth from everyone. People sense what we are or what spirit is within us. When Daniel was brought into a strange land and lived in a heathen land, the king knew he had a different spirit from those around him. King Nebuchadnezzar told Daniel, "I know that the spirit of the holy gods is in thee" (Daniel 4:9).

When the handwriting appeared on the wall during Belshazzar's reign, it was the queen who recognized that Daniel was different from the other wise men in the kingdom and that Daniel had a different set of attitudes from those around him. She said, "There is a man in thy kingdom, in whom is the spirit of the holy gods . . . forasmuch as an excellent spirit, and knowledge, and understanding . . . were found in the same Daniel" (Daniel 5:11-12).

People perceive whether we are holy or not. This happened with the prophet Elisha. He passed through the city of Shunem, and a great woman constrained him to eat bread with her and her husband. Thereafter, every time Elisha passed through the city, he would stop and eat with them. After a while, the woman made her estimation of him. "And she said unto her husband, Behold now, I perceive that this is an holy man of God, which passeth by us continually" (II Kings 4:9).

James Hastings commented, "When the great lady of Shunem speaks of Elisha as 'a holy man of God,' she is not thinking of the saintliness of his character; he is holy, simply as one who stands in a near relation to God."

Holiness Is a Relationship with Christ

When people are made new creatures in Christ Jesus, they are filled with the Holy Spirit of God! The seraphims of heaven know how majestic and holy God is, and they cry, "Holy," in their worship. "And one cried unto another, and said, Holy, holy, holy, is the LORD of hosts: the whole earth is full of his glory" (Isaiah 6:3).

When the Spirit of the holy God truly dwells within us, then He will control our behavior, as we allow Him. We can be Christ-controlled, or Spirit-controlled. Just as a demon-possessed person can be controlled by a demon, so a Spirit-filled person comes under the direct influence of the Holy Spirit, although always with the person's assent and faith.

Behavior is dictated by our mind, spirit, and attitudes. Titus 2:3 gives instruction to women: "The aged women likewise, that they be in behaviour as becometh holiness."

Sometimes God must chasten His children to teach them holiness. Hebrews 12:10 states, "For they [our earthly fathers] verily for a few days chastened us after their own pleasure; but he [God] for our profit, that we might be partakers of his holiness."

God desires for His church to be a part of His holiness. Verses 14-15 continue, "Follow peace with all men, and holiness, without which no man shall see the Lord: looking diligently lest any man fail of the grace of God; lest any root of bitterness springing up trouble you, and thereby many be defiled."

If it is impossible to see the Lord without holiness, why is it that more people do not seek after true holiness? We should note that holiness and the spirit of bitterness are contrasted in the same passage. It is impossible to have holiness if we have a root of bitterness!

What is bitterness? Since it cancels holiness, we must study it. Here are some definitions.

- *Bitter*: painful, distressful, grievous, piercingly cold, characterized by animosity and cruelty, biting, caustic. *Amplified New Testament*: "In order that no root of resentment (rancor, bitterness or hatred) shoot forth."

- *Animosity*: ill will, often resentment, tending

toward hostile action, active enmity, a feeling of antagonism, hostility.

- *Resentment*: a feeling of indignant displeasure because of something regarded as a wrong, insult or the like.

- *Hostility*: state of being hostile, public or private enmity; unfriendliness, animosity.

- *Enmity*: ill will with such as actuates a personal enemy, marked by hatred and antagonism.

- *Rancor*: an old grudge; vehement hatred or ill will; intense malignity or spite; something that nourishes hatred or rankles.

James 5:9 admonishes, "Grudge not one against another, brethren, lest ye be condemned: behold, the judge standeth before the door."

Bitterness is like a cancer that eats at the very core of a person's mind. It is like an acid that burns its container. It is a strong, destroying poison that will sear the brain and deaden spiritual sensitivity. The bitter person will be controlled by hate, resentment, and ill will. He will not be able to think clearly. He will become double-minded in all his ways and eventually be destroyed.

When someone struggles with bitterness, it is good to pray the prayer of David in Psalm 51:7, 10-12: "Purge me with hyssop, and I shall be clean: wash me, and I shall be whiter than snow . . . Create in me a clean heart, O God; and renew a right spirit within me. Cast me not away from thy presence; and take not thy holy spirit from me. Restore unto me the joy of thy salvation; and uphold me with thy free spirit."

When someone harbors bitterness, he is bound and walking around in chains, but when he is washed by God, he exchanges his bondage for a free spirit!

Sooner or later all of us will have a chance to become bitter over something someone did to us or something that was said about us. The choice we must make is whether to be poisoned by the people who did it to us, or whether we will let it go. Someone once said, "When I am bitter, my enemy has me in his pocket." Who has us today? Does God carry us over the rough spots, or does our enemy?

Before the turn of the century, an ardent and dedicated Christian wrote a tract entitled "Come to Jesus." It became famous and influenced many for Christ. Later he became engaged in theological dispute. In reply to a publication by an opponent, he wrote an article bristling with invectives, sharp and cutting as a razor. Looking for a title, he asked his friend. His friend wisely suggested: "Call it 'Go to the Devil' by the author of 'Come to Jesus.'" Instead of publishing the article, he decided to destroy the article.

We must decide whether we are going to live in the Word or in the world. Will the world system dictate to us or will the Word? The Word says to forgive; the world says to get even.

Jacob de Shazer was one of Jimmy Doolittle's raiders who bombed Japan on April 18, 1942. He was an atheist. During the air attack his plane was hit by enemy antiaircraft bullets and he was forced to bail out. He was captured and imprisoned by the Japanese and thought his life was approaching the end. He saw two of his companions shot by a firing squad and saw another die of slow starvation.

During the long months of imprisonment, he pondered the question of why the Japanese hated him and why he hated them. He began to recall some of the things he had heard about Christianity.

Boldly, he asked his jailers if they could get him a Bible. At first they laughed boisterously as at a good joke. Then they grew ugly and warned him to stop making a nuisance of himself. But he kept asking. A year and a half later, in May 1944, a guard finally brought him a Bible, flung it at him, and said, "Three weeks you have. Three weeks, and then I take away." True to his word, in three weeks the guard took the Bible away, and de Shazer never saw it again.

However, in those three weeks of intensive searching, meditating, and delving into the meaning of life and humanity's ultimate destiny, a change came about. Later he was released from Japanese captivity and returned home. In 1948, he and his wife were on their way back to Japan as missionaries. Only God can make this kind of change in a life that has been victimized by the enemy.

The Bible speaks about many different kinds of spirits. Some of them are as follows:

Spirit of bondage	Broken spirit
Spirit of counsel	Spirit of divination
Dumb spirit	Spirit of error
Faithful spirit	Spirit of fear
Foul spirit	Good spirit
Spirit of glory	Spirit of grace
Humble spirit	Spirit of jealousy
Spirit of judgment	Spirit of knowledge
Spirit of meekness	Patient spirit
Perverse spirit	Poor in spirit
Spirit of slumber	Sorrowful spirit
Unclean spirit	Spirit of understanding
Spirit of whoredoms	Spirit of wisdom
Wounded spirit	

Spirit is described as the breath of life, conceived as a kind of breath or vapor animating the body, or in man, mediating between body and soul. It is the agent of vital and conscious functions in man. It is also a mentality, source of perception, and active thought. It is the temper or disposition of mind.

Once when Jesus was on His way to Jerusalem, he sent messengers ahead of Him and told them to prepare a place at Samaria for them to stay. The Samaritans did not like this, because Jesus was only passing through their town, so they refused to give him a place of lodging.

James and John wanted to rain fire down upon the town and burn it up because of their rude treatment of Jesus. "But he turned, and rebuked them, and said, Ye know not what manner of spirit ye are of. For the Son of man is not come to destroy men's lives, but to save them. And they went to another village" (Luke 9:55-56).

When we are followers of Christ, we operate under a different set of laws, because we are born of another spirit. When we are hurt by someone, we do not try to destroy them, but we just keep walking to our next destination in life. We just keep going. We do not take time out to minister judgment.

The question is, "What manner of spirit are you?" Galatians 5:22-23 describes the fruit of the Spirit, listing the attributes that all Christians should strive to attain: "But the fruit of the Spirit is love, joy, peace, longsuffering, gentleness, goodness, faith, meekness, temperance: against such there is no law."

The World's Bible

Christ has no hands but our hands
To do His work today;
He has no feet but our feet
To lead men in His way;
He has no tongues but our tongues
To tell men how He died;
He has no help but our help
To bring them to His side.

We are the only Bible
The careless world will read;
We are the sinner's gospel,
We are the scoffer's creed;
We are the Lord's last message
Given in deed and word—
What if the line is crooked?
What if the type is blurred?

What if our hands are busy
With other work than His?
What if our feet our walking
Where sin's allurement is?
What if our tongues are speaking
Of things His lips would spurn?
How can we hope to help Him
Unless from Him we learn?

—Annie Johnson Flint

CHAPTER FIVE

HOLY IN LOVE

Walter Rauschenbusch gave proper recognition to a virtue that is often missing in this generation:

> One of the glories of Christianity is the place it gives to love. It sums up all religious duty in love to God, and all ethical duty in love to man. It has set before humanity as the fullest revelation of God and the highest expression of manhood the life of Jesus Christ, whose name is a synonym of love. It has made love the dominant characteristic in the nature of God himself, and therewith has written love across the whole universe.[14]

It is God's will for His children to be holy in love towards one another. Ephesians 1:4 states, "According as he hath chosen us in him before the foundation of the world, that we should be holy and without blame before him in love."

John wrote about this love in I John 4:7-10: "Beloved, let us love one another: for love is of God; and every one that loveth is born of God, and knoweth God. He that loveth not knoweth not God; for God is love. In this was manifested the love of God toward us, because that God sent his only begotten Son into the world, that we might live through him. Herein is love, not that we loved God, but that he loved us, and sent his Son to be the propitiation for our sins."

Here is the clincher: "Beloved, if God so loved us, we ought also to love one another. No man hath seen God at any time. If we love one another, God dwelleth in us, and his love is perfected in us" (I John 4:11-12).

John further stated these strong words: "If a man say, I love God, and hateth his brother, he is a liar: for he that loveth not his brother whom he hath seen, how can he love God whom he hath not seen?" (I John 4:20).

So the signpost of holiness is love for one another. If we have a nasty spirit, a hateful attitude, and a gossipy tongue that tears down others, then we are not holy, even though our dress may signal that we are holy. Dress alone is not the plumbline for being holy; it is merely the outgrowth of a holy heart.

Jesus spoke of people who looked holy on the outside and were as dead men's bones on the inside. Let us note in the following passage the superb language He chose to describe people who only looked holy but were in reality filthy on the inside:

"Ye blind guides, which strain at a gnat, and swallow a camel. Woe unto you, scribes and Pharisees, hypocrites! for ye make clean the outside of the cup and of the platter, but within they are full of extortion and excess. Thou blind Pharisee, cleanse first that which is within the cup and platter, that the outside of them may be clean also. Woe unto you, scribes and Pharisees, hypocrites! for ye are like unto whited sepulchres, which indeed appear beautiful outward, but are within full of dead men's bones, and of all uncleanness. Even so ye also outwardly appear righteous unto men, but within ye are full of hypocrisy and iniquity" (Matthew 23:24-28).

What if Jesus told you that you were unclean, blind, an extortionist, a hypocrite, and that you were full of dead men's bones and filled with iniquity? What would you do? Would you repent and change your ways, or would you go on in your own religion, such as the Pharisees did?

Sometimes preachers and church members may get together in certain groups and talk evil of other ministers or saints. When they do so, it is not because they care about holiness standards but because they want to tear someone down so they will look good in the eyes of the persons to whom they are speaking. It is not a love for truth that propels them, it is a love for self. Jealousy coats their bones, and they send out a green pollution of gossip that hurts and wounds an innocent party. While this may be done in the name of holiness, it is not holiness; it is putrefying!

Beware of people who speak evil of others and try to tear them down. Nine times out of ten what they are saying is embellished lies. The person talked about never gets to explain his story or even defend himself. Walls are built, families are hurt, and churches are emptied—all because of heartless gossip.

Like the Pharisees and scribes of Jesus' day, some people are more in love with their standards than they are with God. They are mean spirited, and they hurt people, instead of winning them with love and mercy. On the inside of them is the rattle of dead bones. They are a menace to the kingdom of God!

God desires for the church to "put on therefore, as the elect of God, holy and beloved, bowels of mercies, kindness, humbleness of mind, meekness, longsuffering; forbearing one another, and forgiving one another, if any man have a quarrel against any: even as Christ forgave you, so also do ye. And above all these things put on charity, which is the bond of perfectness" (Colossians 3:12-14).

Let us examine more closely the things that God wants His people to do.

Things to Put On

- *Bowels*: the seat of pity or kindness.
- *Mercy*: forbearance from inflicting harm, espe-

cially when one has the power to inflict it; compassionate treatment of an offender of adversary; disposition to exercise compassion or forgiveness; compassionate treatment of the unfortunate and helpless.

- *Kindness*: state or quality of being kind; disposed to do good and confer happiness; benevolent; sympathetic; gracious; proceeding from or characterized by goodness, gentleness, love.

- *Humble*: not proud or assertive in spirit towards others; unpretentious; not pretending; not thinking more highly of self than one ought.

- *Meek*: mild of temper; not easily provoked or irritated; patient under injuries; not vain, haughty, or resentful.

- *Longsuffering*: long and patient endurance of offense.

Do This Also

- *Forbearing*: refraining from the enforcement of what is due; indulgence toward offenders or enemies; longsuffering; bearing with or enduring; restraining oneself from expressing, exacting, punishing, or injuring others.

- *Forgiving*: ceasing to feel resentment against, on account of wrong committed; giving up claim to requital (revenge) from or retribution (punishment) upon (an offender); pardoning.

Above All, Put On This

- *Charity*: the virtue or act of loving God with a love that transcends that for creatures, and of loving others for the sake of God; love in its perfection; rendering of Greek *agape* in the New Testament.

This brings us to the question, What is love? If charity is a step up from natural love, what is love in its perfection? The best description is found in I Corinthians 13:4-8:

- "Charity suffereth long": patient endurance of offense.

- "Charity is kind": loving, benevolent, helping others.

- "Charity vaunteth not itself": does not talk about or elevate self continually.

- "Charity is not puffed up": is humble.

- "Doth not behave itself unseemly": does not

embarrass or act unbecoming.

- "Seeketh not her own": seeks welfare of others.
- "Is not easily provoked": temper is under control.
- "Thinketh no evil": thinks only good about others.
- "Rejoiceth not in iniquity": does not delight in wickedness or sins.
- "Rejoiceth in the truth": delights in God's Word.
- "Beareth all things": is cheerful and uncomplaining in a trial.
- "Believeth all things": believes that God is in control.
- "Hopeth all things": does not give up, but hopes in God.
- "Endureth all things": patient in the things that God allows.
- "Charity never faileth": continues to love, no matter what.

This is a large order for any Christian to attain. It is easy to see that we must put away the pointing finger, for there is so much for each of us to work on in our own lives.

The Bible speaks about the negative aspects of pointing a finger at other people, picking out their flaws and shining a bad light on them. Isaiah 58:9 gives a promise, but only if one gives up the judgment of others: "Then shalt thou call, and the Lord shall answer; thou shalt cry, and he shall say, Here I am. If thou take away from the midst of thee the yoke, the putting forth of the finger, and speaking vanity." There is an *if* that the Lord requires: it is putting away the pointing of the finger, or judging others. "Judge not, that ye be not judged" (Matthew 7:1).

I Peter 1:22 talks about the purification of love: "Seeing ye have purified your souls in obeying the truth through the Spirit unto unfeigned [sincere, genuine, not hypocritical] love of the brethren, see that ye love one another with a pure heart fervently [glowing, burning with love, warm in feeling, love passionately]."

Ephesians 5:2 instructs the followers of God to walk in love: "And walk in love, as Christ also hath loved us, and hath given himself for us an offering and a sacrifice to God for a sweetsmelling savour."

Love for each other is a sacrifice given back to God, and it becomes a sweet smell in His nostrils. He accepts the offering. It was He who gave love first to His children. All He asks is that they give it back to Him by loving Him and one another. Two passages of Scripture that teach this truth are as follows:

"And hope maketh not ashamed; because the love of

God is shed abroad in our hearts by the Holy Ghost which is given unto us" (Romans 5:5).

"And Jesus answered him, The first of all the commandments is, Hear, O Israel; The Lord our God is one Lord: and thou shalt love the Lord thy God with all thy heart, and with all thy soul, and with all thy mind, and with all thy strength: this is the first commandment. And the second is like, namely this, Thou shalt love thy neighbour as thyself. There is none other commandment greater than these" (Mark 12:29-31).

When people receive the Holy Ghost, they are filled with God's love. That is why it is important to stay full of the Holy Ghost and not let it "leak out." It takes daily prayer to stay full of the Spirit. If we want to fill something up that has been emptied out, we must go back to the source from which we received it.

Jude 18-21 shows the difference between those who are filled with the Spirit and those who are without it: "They told you there should be mockers in the last time, who should walk after their own ungodly lusts. These be they who separate themselves, sensual, having not the Spirit. But ye, beloved, building up yourselves on your most holy faith, praying in the Holy Ghost, keep yourselves in the love of God, looking for the mercy of our Lord Jesus Christ unto eternal life."

Let us notice the following highlights of this passage:

- There are those who will walk after their own ungodly lusts.

- They separate themselves from the Spirit and are sensual. People who are without God's love, which is placed in their heart by the Holy Ghost, are sensual.

- But Christians will build themselves up by praying in the Holy Ghost.

- Keep yourselves in the love of God. To keep something means that it must be maintained and guarded with careful observance.

God desires for all Christians to abound in love one toward another and be blameless in holiness. He couples love and holiness together in I Thessalonians 3:12-13: "And the Lord make you to increase and abound in love one toward another, and toward all men, even as we do toward you: to the end he may stablish your hearts unblameable in holiness before God, even our Father, at the coming of our Lord Jesus Christ with all his saints."

"Abound in love toward . . . all men" is a commandment! Jesus gave the following instructions in Luke 6:35-36: "But love ye your enemies, and do good, and lend, hoping for nothing again; and your reward shall be great, and ye shall be the children of the Highest: for he is kind unto the unthankful and to the evil. Be ye therefore merciful, as your Father also is merciful."

What are we going to do with these truths? Are we going to be haughty, pull our self-righteous robes around us, and be rude and uncaring to evil ones? Are we willing to obey *all* the Scriptures, or will we pick and choose what feels good?

Susan Fahncke chose to obey these verses of Scripture. I received her story by e-mail. The following account is definitely food for thought:

> He was kind of scary. He sat there on the grass with his cardboard sign, his dog (actually his dog was adorable), and tattoos running up and down both arms and even on his neck. His sign proclaimed him to be "stuck and hungry" and to please help.
>
> I'm a sucker for anyone needing help. My husband both hates and loves this quality in me. I pulled the van over and in my rear view mirror contemplated this man, tattoos and all. He was youngish, maybe forty. He wore one of those bandannas tied over his head, biker/pirate style. Anyone could see he was dirty and had a scraggly beard. But if you looked closer, you could see that he had neatly tucked in the black T-shirt, and his things were in a small, tidy bundle. Nobody was stopping for him. I could see the other drivers take one look and immediately focus on something else.
>
> It was so hot. I could see in the man's very blue eyes how dejected and tired and worn out he felt. The sweat was trickling down his face. As

I sat with the air conditioning blowing, the verse of Scripture suddenly popped into my head: "Inasmuch as ye have done it unto one of the least of these my brethren, ye have done it unto me."

I reached down into my purse and extracted a ten-dollar bill. My twelve-year-old son, Nick, knew right away what I was doing. "Can I take it to him, Mom?"

"Be careful, honey," I warned and handed him the money. I watched in the mirror as he rushed over to the man and, with a shy smile, handed it to him. I saw the man, startled, stand and take the money, putting it into his back pocket. Good, I thought to myself. Now he will at least have a hot meal tonight. I felt satisfied, proud of myself. I had made a sacrifice, and now I could go on with my errands.

When Nick got back into the car, he looked at me with sad, pleading eyes. "Mom, his dog looks so hot and the man is really nice." I knew I had to do more. "Go back and tell him to stay there, that we will be back in fifteen minutes," I told Nick. He bounded out of the car and ran to tell the tattooed stranger.

We then ran to the nearest store and bought our gifts carefully. "It can't be too heavy," I explained to the children. "He has to be able to carry it around with him." We finally settled on our purchases. A bag of Ol' Roy, a flavored chew-toy shaped like a bone, a water dish, bacon-flavored snacks (for the dog), two bottles of water (one for the dog, one for Mr. Tattoos), and some people snacks for the man.

We rushed back to the spot where we had left him, and there he was, still waiting. And still nobody else was stopping for him. With hands shaking, I grabbed our bags and climbed out of the car, all four of my children following me, each carrying gifts. As we walked up to him, I had a fleeting moment of fear, hoping he wasn't a serial killer. I looked into his eyes and saw something that startled me and made me ashamed of my judgment. I saw tears. He was fighting like a little boy to hold back his tears. How long had it been since someone showed this man kindness? I told him I hoped it wasn't too heavy for him to carry and showed him what we had bought. He stood there, like a child at Christmas, and I felt like my small contributions were so inadequate.

When I took out the water dish, he snatched it out of my hands as if it were solid gold and told me he had had no way to give his dog water. He gingerly set it down, filled it with the bottled water we brought, and stood up to look directly into my eyes. His were so blue, so intense, and my own filled with tears as he said, "Ma'am, I don't know what to say." He then put both hands on his bandanna-clad head and just started to cry. This man, this "scary" man, was so gentle, so sweet and humble.

I smiled through my tears and said, "Don't say anything." Then I noticed the tattoo on his neck. It said, "Mamma tried." As we all piled into the van and drove away, he was on his knees, arms around his dog, kissing his nose and smiling. I waved cheerfully and then fully broke down in tears.

I have so much. My worries seem so trivial and petty now. I have a home, a loving husband, four beautiful children. I have a bed. I wondered where he would sleep tonight. My stepdaughter, Brandie, turned to me and said in the sweetest little-girl voice. "I feel so good."

Although it seemed as if we had helped him, the man with the tattoos gave us a gift that I will never forget. He taught that no matter what the outside looks like, inside each of us is a human being deserving of kindness and compassion. He opened my heart.

There is a hurting world that is waiting for the church to obey the Scriptures. They are in the prisons, by the side of the road, in the grocery stores, in the executive offices, on the airplanes, in the banks; they are everywhere just waiting on the church to really care.

Jesus said, "For I was an hungred, and ye gave me no

meat: I was thirsty, and ye gave me no drink: I was a stranger, and ye took me not in: naked, and ye clothed me not: sick, and in prison, and ye visited me not. Then shall they also answer him, saying, Lord, when saw we thee an hungred, or athirst, or a stranger, or naked, or sick, or in prison, and did not minister unto thee? Then shall he answer them, saying, Verily I say unto you, Inasmuch as ye did it not to one of the least of these, ye did it not to me. And these shall go away into everlasting punishment: but the righteous into life eternal" (Matthew 25:42-46). The people who fed the hungry, clothed the needy, visited the sick and visited the prisoners, He called righteous. The people who did not minister to others, He sent into everlasting punishment.

Maybe the reason the church has so many factions and divisions and people who are miserable is because instead of giving, they are grabbing for themselves; instead of reaching out to others, they are busy tearing one another apart.

We should remember that I Thessalonians 3:12 commands us to "increase and abound in love one toward another, and toward all men." *This includes the whole world: red, yellow, brown, black, and white!*

The Inner Life

There is no room for a complainer in a universe of law, and worry is soul-suicide. By your very attitude of mind you are strengthening the chains which bind you, and are drawing about you the darkness by which you are enveloped. Alter your outlook upon life, and your outward life will alter. Build yourself up in the faith and knowledge, and make yourself worthy of better surroundings and wider opportunities. Be sure, first of all, that you are making the best of what you have. Do not delude yourself into supposing that you can step into greater advantages whilst overlooking smaller ones, for if you could, the advantage would be impermanent and you would quickly fall back again in order to learn the lesson which you had neglected.

—James Allen

CHAPTER SIX

HOLY IN SPEECH

God desires that the glory of heaven would be found in our words. Ephesians 1:12 is God's will for us: "That we should be to the praise of his glory, who first trusted in Christ."

A call from heaven is signaling all Christians to keep their conversation holy. I Peter 1:14-16 states: "As obedient children, not fashioning yourselves according to the former lusts in your ignorance: but as he which hath called you is holy, so be ye holy in all manner of conversation; because it is written, Be ye holy; for I am holy."

We are to be holy in all manner of conversation, or conduct. We should note the before and after. Before: vain conversation (I Peter 1:18). After: holy conversation (I Peter 1:15).

The command to have holy conversation is reiterated

in II Peter 3:11, and it has to do with the time of the coming of the Lord, which is near: "Seeing then that all these things shall be dissolved, what manner of persons ought ye to be in all holy conversation and godliness."

Psalm 50:23 promises, "Whoso offereth praise glorifieth me: and to him that ordereth his conversation aright will I shew the salvation of God." Our conversations should be ordered; we should not just open our mouths without thinking.

Most people talk too much. They let the words fly and then are tormented by having said too much. "If only I hadn't said that," is often the aftermath of many conversations. That is why Christians are instructed to learn to be quiet.

Study to Be Quiet

"And that ye study to be quiet, and to do your own business, and to work with your own hands, as we commanded you" (I Thessalonians 4:11).

William Osler, M.D., wrote:

> To know when to keep silent is one of the finest of arts. The atmosphere of life is darkened by murmuring and whispering over the non-essentials, the trifles that are inevitably incident to the hurly-burly of the day's routine. Things cannot always go our way. Learn to accept in silence the minor aggravations. Cultivate the gift of quietude and consume your own smoke with an extra

> draught of hard work so that those about you may not be annoyed with the dust and soot of your complaints.[15]

Paul could testify of the good conduct of his life: "For our rejoicing is this, the testimony of our conscience, that in simplicity and godly sincerity, not with fleshly wisdom, but by the grace of God, we have had our conversation in the world, and more abundantly to you-ward" (II Corinthians 1:12). The world did not affect his conduct; God did!

Speak Only the Truth

H. A. Ironside told the following humorous story that illustrates what can happen when people speak without truth:

> Half the scandal that goes around among members of the Church is simply the result of jumping at conclusions. Not long ago I read a little article in a church bulletin in which the pastor explained that he had been greatly troubled by a rumor going around to the effect that his wife had attended a meeting of some heretical group and that he had gone there in great indignation and dragged her out by the hair of her head and brought her home and beat her. He undertook to explain that he had not dragged his wife out of that meeting, that he had never at any time

> dragged her about by the hair, and that he had never beaten her, and also that his wife had never attended that meeting, and finally that he was a bachelor and had never had a wife.[16]

Ephesians 4:25 admonishes Christians to speak truth: "Wherefore putting away lying, speak every man truth with his neighbour: for we are members one of another."

I Peter 2:12 states, "Having your conversation honest among the Gentiles: that, whereas they speak against you as evildoers, they may by your good works, which they shall behold, glorify God in the day of visitation."

People who seek sincerely after God, do their best to live a clean life, and order all their conduct, including their conversation, in the Word, will be respected by the world. The world will see the glory of God resting upon them.

Psalm 119:133 is a prayer any sincere Christian should pray daily: "Order my steps in thy word: and let not any iniquity have dominion over me."

Learn to Speak Softly When There Is Anger

Ephesians 4:26 says, "Be ye angry, and sin not," and it comes right before a verse connected with the tongue. Ephesians 4:29-31 continues to deal with the tongue: "Let no corrupt communication proceed out of your mouth, but that which is good to the use of edifying, that it may minister grace unto the hearers. And grieve not the holy Spirit of God, whereby ye are sealed unto the day of redemption. Let all bitterness, and wrath, and anger, and clamour, and evil speaking, be put away from you, with all malice."

Let us examine the words used here that concern the tongue or have an effect on a person's speech.

- *Corrupt*: changed from a state of uprightness, correctness, and truth to a bad state; depraved, debased, and perverted.
- *Grace*: favor, kindness, and good will.
- *Edify*: to build up or construct; to teach or improve.
- *Bitterness*: something painful, distressing, grievous, piercingly cold, sharp and galling.
- *Wrath*: violent anger, vehement exasperation, resentful rage, fury.
- *Anger*: (noun) a strong passion or emotion of displeasure and usually antagonism; (verb) to distress, provoke and enrage.
- *Clamour*: a loud and continued shouting or exclamation of dissatisfaction or discontent.
- *Evil speaking*: speech that tends to injury and

mischief, that produces or threatens sorrow, distress, or calamity.

- *Malice*: enmity of heart, malevolence, ill-will, spite, badness.

We should also note how the chapter ends: "And be ye kind one to another, tenderhearted, forgiving one another, even as God for Christ's sake hath forgiven you" (Ephesians 4:32).

MAKE IT UP

Life is too short for grievances
For quarrels and for tears.
What's the use of wasting
Precious days and precious tears?

If there's something to forgive,
Forgive without delay.
Maybe you, too, were part to blame,
So make it up today.

Be generous—forget the past
And take the broader view;
Cast away all bitterness and
Let the sunshine through.

If it's within your power

A broken heart to mend,
Remember—love is all that
Really matters—in the end.[17]

Those with Righteous Hearts Think before They Speak

Proverbs 15:28 says, "The heart of the righteous studieth to answer: but the mouth of the wicked poureth out evil things."

James 3:13 states that a wise man will reveal his wisdom in his behavior: "Who is a wise man and endued with knowledge among you? let him shew out of a good conversation his works with meekness of wisdom."

Walter B. Knight told the following story about an infuriated woman who called him on the phone one day, and what he did about it:

> Hardly had I said, "Hello," when she began to slander a fine Christian couple. I quickly switched the receiver from my ear to my kneecap. The angry woman spoke so animatedly and loud that I could hear her voice, although I didn't get what she was saying. Finally she became silent.
>
> Then I lifted the receiver from my kneecap to my ear and asked softly, "Is there anything else?"
>
> "Well, I guess not," she replied. It was evident that she had cooled off considerably. The soft answer seemed to turn away what unspent wrath was left in her. As I cradled the receiver, I said,

"Thank God, I didn't let my ear be used as a garbage can."[18]

Speak to Yourself Good Things

Ephesians 5:19-20 instructs those who are filled with the Spirit of God as follows: "Speaking to yourselves in psalms and hymns and spiritual songs, singing and making melody in your heart to the Lord; giving thanks always for all things unto God and the Father in the name of our Lord Jesus Christ."

The reason why there are so many miserable, unhappy Christians is that they are speaking to themselves about how someone wronged them, how they were ignored or rejected, how they were gossiped about, or how to get even with those who spoke against them.

Think about it. Do inventory in your own thought patterns. Do you obey Ephesians 5:19-20? Do you speak psalms to yourself? Do you sing songs and make melody unto the Lord? Do you give thanks for all things, no matter how they hurt you? Is the church really obeying the Scriptures, or is she living in the flesh, going according to her own ways? How powerful the church would become if she obeyed *all* the Bible and not just gain entrance to the kingdom of God!

Speak Clean Words

Ephesians 5:3-6 puts filthy words in the same text with fornication and uncleanness: "But fornication, and all uncleanness, or covetousness, let it not be once named among you, as becometh saints; neither filthiness, nor foolish talking, nor jesting, which are not convenient: but rather giving of thanks. For this ye know, that no whoremonger, nor unclean person, nor covetous man, who is an idolater, hath any inheritance in the kingdom of Christ and of God. Let no man deceive you with vain words."

A "jest" is a story or idle tale, a jeering or satirical remark, an occurrence or saying provocative of merriment; a joke. Here it has the connotation of a dirty joke. It may seem like a small thing, but words affect our destiny.

A woman shared with me a sad story of how dirty jokes led to the breakup of her marriage. It started out by her husband listening to other friends who would tell off-color jokes with sexual overtones or innuendoes. He was a minister and should have taken a stand against these jokes, but instead he just laughed at them. Then he started telling the jokes. Next he was joined by some others who came over to his house, and they all went to a magazine shop downtown to look at pornographic magazines. First he heard, then he talked, and then he looked, but he was not satisfied until he experienced it. Lust was conceived, and it brought about the death of her marriage. It was discovered that he had three women at one time. The situation started so slyly and then just became a river of filth.

Ephesians 2:2-3 describes what happened here:

"Wherein in time past ye walked according to the course of this world, according to the prince of the power of the air, the spirit that now worketh in the children of disobedience: among whom also we all had our conversation in times past in the lusts of our flesh, fulfilling the desires of the flesh and of the mind; and were by nature the children of wrath, even as others."

I want to insert here a word of warning to all men and women. Make up your mind now: refuse to dabble in pornography. Do not take even a peek at the evil that is displayed on the Internet. We are "dead with Christ from the rudiments of the world" (Colossians 2:20).

The United States is the world's leading producer of pornography and the largest consumer of child pornography. Considering the millions of abortions and the flood of pornography, an ocean of filth is flowing through our streets and into the homes. Someone must stand up and stop the flood.

It is time to change any conversation that is unclean or suggestive. Ephesians 4:22-24 commands: "That ye put off concerning the former conversation the old man, which is corrupt according to the deceitful lusts; and be renewed in the spirit of your mind; and that ye put on the new man, which after God is created in righteousness and true holiness." True holiness encompasses both the tongue and the mind!

Speak Pleasant Words

Proverbs 16:23-24 states, "The heart of the wise teacheth his mouth, and addeth learning to his lips. Pleasant words are as an honeycomb, sweet to the soul, and health to the bones."

There is too much sickness among Christians. Some of it could be alleviated if there was more pleasant talk and less gossip, murmuring, criticism, and complaining.

The Bible says that pleasant words are health to the bones. The bones are essential to good health, because that is where the bone marrow is. The yellow marrow is found in the cavities of long bones, and the red marrow is found in the cancellous tissue of various bones. This is where the red blood corpuscles are formed. Thus, many diseases can arise if the bones are not healthy. In short, our attitude and speech are important to our health, so we must be careful what we speak!

Proverbs 27:9 says, "Ointment and perfume rejoice the heart: so doth the sweetness of a man's friend by hearty counsel." Sweet words of a friend rejoice the heart!

Put Away Murmuring, Complaining, Backbiting, and Whispering

Murmuring is complaining in a low, muttering voice; repining; grumbling; expressing discontent in a low, continued noise.

Philippians 2:14-15 instructs: "Do all things without murmurings and disputings: that ye may be blameless and harmless, the sons of God, without rebuke, in the midst of a crooked and perverse nation, among whom ye shine as lights in the world."

I Corinthians 10:10 similarly admonishes, "Neither murmur ye, as some of them also murmured, and were destroyed of the destroyer."

This passage of Scripture refers to the murmuring of the Israelites. When they murmured in the wilderness against Moses and Aaron because they had no meat or bread to eat, Moses told them they were murmuring against God. "And Moses said, This shall be, when the LORD shall give you in the evening flesh to eat, and in the morning bread to the full; for that the LORD heareth your murmurings which ye murmur against him: and what are we? your murmurings are not against us, but against the LORD" (Exodus 16:8).

Then God spoke. "And the LORD spake unto Moses, saying, I have heard the murmurings of the children of Israel: speak unto them, saying, At even ye shall eat flesh, and in the morning ye shall be filled with bread; and ye shall know that I am the LORD your God" (Exodus 16:11-12).

They continued to murmur about everything until God finally said to them: "How long shall I bear with this evil congregation, which murmur against me? I have heard the murmurings of the children of Israel, which they murmur against me. Say unto them, As truly as I live, saith the LORD, as ye have spoken in mine ears, so will I do to you: your carcases shall fall in this wilderness; and all that were numbered of you, according to your whole number" (Numbers 14:27-29).

Complaining means giving utterance to grief, pain,

discontent; lamenting and murmuring; making a formal accusation or charge.

In the story of Job, the Bible says that "in all this Job sinned not, nor charged God foolishly" (Job 1:22).

God hates complaining, as Numbers 11:1-2 reveals: "And when the people complained, it displeased the LORD: and the LORD heard it; and his anger was kindled; and the fire of the LORD burnt among them, and consumed them that were in the uttermost parts of the camp. And the people cried unto Moses; and when Moses prayed unto the LORD, the fire was quenched."

In Jude 16, God had a word to say about apostate teachers who spoke evil of dignities and were complainers: "These are murmurers, complainers, walking after their own lusts; and their mouth speaketh great swelling words, having men's persons in admiration because of advantage."

There was once a woman who had been broken by a great tragedy in her life. She had been living under the crushing weight of a heavy burden for so long that praise had given way to complaint. Finally she cried out in bitterness of soul, "Oh, I would to God I had never been made!"

In response to her rebellious words a friend wisely replied, "Why, my dear child, you are not made yet; you are only being made, and you are quarreling with God's process."

I Peter 5:10 talks about being made: "But the God of all grace, who hath called us unto his eternal glory by

Christ Jesus, after that ye have suffered a while, make you perfect, stablish, strengthen, settle you."

Backbiting means censuring meanly or reviling one who is absent; slandering or speaking evil of.

Romans 1:29-31 gives a list of those who did not glorify God as God. Because of this, God gave them up to vile affections (passions): "Being filled with all unrighteousness, fornication, wickedness, covetousness, maliciousness; full of envy, murder, debate, deceit, malignity; whisperers, backbiters, haters of God, despiteful, proud, boasters, inventors of evil things, disobedient to parents, without understanding, covenantbreakers, without natural affection, implacable, unmerciful." We should note that backbiting is listed along with murder.

When the question was asked as to who would abide in the Lord's tabernacle, the Lord answered the question in four verses. One of those verses deals with backbiting. Psalm 15:3 says, "He that backbiteth not with his tongue, nor doeth evil to his neighbour, not taketh up a reproach against his neighbour."

Paul was concerned about backbiting entering into the church. "For I fear, lest, when I come, I shall not find you such as I would, and that I shall be found unto you such as ye would not: lest there be debates, envyings, wraths, strifes, backbitings, whisperings, swellings, tumults" (II Corinthians 12:20).

Proverbs 28:25 says, "He that is of a proud heart stirreth up strife."

Whispering is speaking softly, or under the breath, to

be heard only by one; speaking covertly, especially in conspiracy or criticism.

Psalm 41:7 says, "All that hate me whisper together against me: against me do they devise my hurt." Proverbs 16:28 states, "A froward man soweth strife: and a whisperer separateth chief friends."

As we have already seen in Romans 1:29, whisperers are listed with those who did not glorify God and He cut them off. Whisperings are also listed among the things that Paul warned the church about in II Corinthians 12:20.

Proverbs 6:16-19 Lists Seven Things That God Hates

"These six things doth the LORD hate: yea, seven are an abomination unto him." These things are:

- A proud look
- A lying tongue
- Hands that shed innocent blood
- A heart that deviseth wicked imaginations
- Feet that be swift in running to mischief
- A false witness that speaketh lies
- He that soweth discord

Discord is the absence of unity; disagreement; hence, contention, strife, conflict. In music it is harsh or jarring, as a *discordant* notes or sounds.

Do Not Gossip!

"Where no wood is, there the fire goeth out: so where there is no talebearer, the strife ceaseth. As coals are to burning coals, and wood to fire; so is a contentious man to kindle strife. The words of a talebearer are as wounds, and they go down into the innermost parts of the belly" (Proverbs 26:20-22).

Words Affect Our Destiny

Jesus spoke in Matthew 12:36-37 about the power of words: "But I say unto you, That every idle word that men shall speak, they shall give account thereof in the day of judgment. For by thy words thou shalt be justified, and by thy words thou shalt be condemned."

Because words affect our destiny, we must determine to speak clean, positive words that do not hurt us or anyone. Philippians 1:27 says of our conduct: "Only let your conversation be as it becometh the gospel of Christ."

Our Speech Influences Others

I Timothy 4:12 admonishes us to be an example: "Let no man despise thy youth; but be thou an example of the believers, in word, in conversation, in charity, in spirit, in faith, in purity."

People listen to what we say. They notice whether our

words are clean, sincere and uplifting, or whether they crush. Let us examine our speech and conduct in the light of God's Word!

More than seeking to be an example of good speech and conduct, let us go out of our way to minister grace to those who are hurting. The following poem says it well:

You entered my life in a casual way
And saw at a glance what I needed;
There were others who passed me or met me each day,
But never a one of them heeded.
Perhaps you were thinking of other folks more,
Or chance simply seemed to decree it;
I know there were many such chances before,
But the others—well, they didn't see it.

You said just the thing that I wished you would say,
And you made me believe that you meant it;
I held up my head in the old gallant way
And resolved you should never repent it.
There are times when encouragement means such a lot,
And a word is enough to convey it;
There were others who could have, as easy as not—
But, just the same, they didn't say it.

There may have been someone who could have done more

To help me along, though I doubt it;
What I needed was cheering, and always before,
They had let me plod onward without it.
You helped to refashion the dream of my heart
And made me turn eagerly to it;
There were others who might have (I question that part),
But, after all, they didn't do it!

—Grace Stricker Dawson

Peculiar

But there is such a thing as being so deeply
Imbued with the Spirit of God, that you
Must and will act so as to appear strange
And eccentric, to those who cannot
Understand the reasons of your
Conduct.

—Charles G. Finney

CHAPTER SEVEN

HOLY IN DRESS

The statement has often been made, "God doesn't care what people wear." This is totally untrue! He does care what people wear.

Satan came disguised as an angel of light in the Garden of Eden and attacked the thoughts and mind of Eve with his question, "Hath God said?" Then he said, in essence, "God has only told you not to eat of this fruit because He does not want you to be as intelligent as He. If you eat of the fruit, then you will become as gods and know good and evil. Your eyes will be opened into a new world, and you will not die."

Eve looked and concluded three things: that the tree was good for food, that it was pleasant to the eyes, and that it was desired to make one wise. For her, the tree contained sustenance, gratification, and wisdom. So she ate of the tree. God's voice was silenced by the voice of Satan. She listened more to what Satan said than what God said. Her mind was beguiled by the tricks of the enemy.

People are still listening to the voice of the enemy. They are selling their soul for the beggarly elements of the world system. Fashion designers and Hollywood pump out new styles that say, "It is good, it is pleasant to the eyes, and it will make you fit in with what the famous designers have concocted."

When only humans have the say about what we wear, we will never understand the will of God on the subject. We must hear the final word from God.

What does God say about our clothes? He said something about the clothes that Adam and Eve put on in the garden. Because their eyes were opened, they saw that they were naked, so they sewed fig leaves together and covered their nakedness, but this was not enough for God.

When God walked through the garden at His usual meeting time with Adam, Adam was not to be found. God called, "Adam, where art thou?" Adam said, "I heard thy voice in the garden, and I was afraid, because I was naked; and I hid myself." (See Genesis 3:10.) God asked him who told him that he was naked. The story came forth from Adam's lips of the disobedience of him and his wife. They had eaten of the tree of the knowledge of good and evil.

God pronounced judgment upon them and upon

Satan, then He made coats of skins and clothed them. After that He drove them out of the Garden of Eden and placed cherubims with a flaming sword at the entrance to the garden. Man could no longer go into the garden and eat of the tree of life.

There was no need for clothes until the sin of disobedience entered the garden. The fashion scene began because of this sin. Satan has been trying to rule the minds of men and women ever since this time.

The question is, Who is going to clothe us—God or self? Will God's Word be our guide, or will the world system dictate to us? Fashions come and go, but we must measure all fashions for God's children by the guidebook of heaven. If they pass this test, then they are all right to wear. If there is the slightest hint of any immodesty in these fashions, or if they take away from the glory that God wants to rest upon His children, then they need to be discarded.

In the garden, Adam and Eve's clothing betrayed their spiritual condition. Before their sin, there was no need for clothing, but after their sin, they knew instinctively that they had to be covered. When sin came, the beautiful bodies that God created in glory and honor were subjected to dishonor and weakness. (See I Corinthians 15:43.) Temptation entered the human race, and because all men and women became sinners subject to the temptations of the flesh, it became needful to clothe our bodies.

God was not only interested in what Adam and Eve

wore, but He has given strict details all through the Scriptures on how to dress. He gave instructions on what the priests were to wear in the Tabernacle and in the Temple. He even told them how to make them and what color the clothing was to be.

He told the women of the Jewish nation not to wear men's apparel in Deuteronomy 22:5. Recently while I was speaking at a women's prayer conference in southern California, a discussion about the question of women wearing pants arose at the table where I was sitting. Two interesting stories emerged.

One woman told about shopping in the garment district in Los Angeles with her sister who was a pastor's wife. They were trying to find a suit with length enough to cover the knees and were having difficulty doing so. One of the saleswomen said how nice a certain suit would look on her. Finally the woman just told her outright, "She is a pastor's wife, and she needs to find a suit that covers the knees."

The saleswoman replied, "Oh, the Jewish women come in here all the time with the same request. If they like a suit that is too short, they will have the seamstress add length at the waistline, which is covered by the jacket. That way they get their modest skirt length."

After this story was shared, another woman joined in with another story. She told about being at Knott's Berry Farm, an amusement park near Los Angeles, where she saw some girls wearing long jean skirts. She tried to get close enough to see if there was a brand name on them.

Because they were so attractive, she wanted to get some for her girls.

She finally asked one of the women, who seemed to be a chaperone of the girls, why they all wore long skirts instead of pants. The women responded by saying that they were following the instruction of the Bible and the custom of the Jewish people. They had adhered to this teaching from generation to generation. Their women simply did not wear pants because they were instructed not to wear them many centuries ago.

Discussion followed about the Jewish people, and someone informed us that there was a strong Jewish settlement in that area and that not only were they strict in their dress codes but they were also strict in their eating and dietary laws. One of the women at the table told us that she went there to buy the meat she used for her family.

Long after the discussion had ceased, I pondered the information. The longer I thought about it, the more excited I became. These were the people who had received the original instructions on how women were to dress, and they were still keeping those guidelines, even in a crazy, mixed-up world of confusion, filth, and suggestive dress. My heart swelled in thankfulness for a people who were willing to stand up for the truth of God's Word.

Modesty of dress is carried over into the New Testament and commanded in the New Testament church, which is under the new dispensation of grace. God still instructs the women how to dress. Some women have said, "Nobody is going to tell me how to dress." That is the same spirit of rebellion that entered into the Garden of Eden and caused Adam and Eve to be cast out of the garden. "Rebellion is as the sin of witchcraft" (I Samuel 15:23), and it will lead people on a downward trail every time.

I say, "God, teach me how to dress, because I want Your approval." God's thoughts are above our thoughts, and His ways are above our ways. (See Isaiah 55:8-9.) He knows all things from the end to the beginning, so why should we not trust Him to give us guidelines for clothing ourselves? He wants His children to be well-groomed, clean, and beautiful, but modest. So what does God say about fashion?

God wants Satan and all people to know to whom we belong—whose team we represent. In 1987, while I was attending Delta College, a prominent TV personality and his wife were in the newspaper headlines. They were under question for possible tax evasion and other things. One morning in class, a discussion arose about this couple. Some of the students said that the wife's appearance did not shape up to being a Christian.

One of the girls who had bleached, spiked hair, wore a leather miniskirt, and was layered with much makeup, made the statement about the wife: "She looks like a harlot." Back and forth, the students hotly discussed this couple who happened to be in the news at that time. I was sitting there quietly, not saying a word.

Suddenly one of the boys jumped out of his seat and

ran across the room to where I was. He stood above me, pointed his finger down at me, and said loudly for everyone in the room to hear, "You want to know what a Christian should look like? Joy Haney looks like a Christian."

It warmed my heart that they could tell to whom I belonged. I thought, They can look how they want to look—and some of them look pretty wild—but if you say you are a Christian, then the world expects you to look like one.

People in everyday life are often identified by the uniform they wear. We know a fireman by the hat he wears, the policeman by the clothes he wears, the nurse, the airline pilot, the stewardess, the prisoner—they are all identified by their clothing. People are set apart or separated from other people by clothing. What they wear denotes position, rank, and identification.

In the sports world, the uniform of a team is very important. It would be impossible to play and win if the opposing teams did not wear different uniforms. It is imperative that they be identified, and that is done by what they wear. It is with a sense of pride that they don the uniform.

Even film producers know the power of dress. When they want to portray a certain character, they dress them accordingly. In the early days of television, the villain and the good guys were identified by a certain look and the way they dressed.

Not only does people's dress identify them, but it

also reveals how they feel about themselves and their surroundings. America has deteriorated in her morals, and the decline is displayed in the way she dresses. The way people dress signals how they feel inside.

The attitude of rebellion was displayed in the era when protesters burned the flag of the United States of America. They wore faded blue jeans with frayed edges. They grew beards. They did not bathe, wash their hair, or use deodorant. They stitched the United States flag upside down on their sleeves. They made a statement by the way they dressed. They were saying, "My clothing shows my contempt for what America has always stood for."

Several years back there was a book entitled *Dress for Success*. Throughout the book, the author emphasized that the way we dress paves the way for greater things. There has been talk about the "power suit." Others have discussed certain colors that speak of authority and rank. Two of the power colors that are supposed to signify authority are black and navy. That is probably why many stewardesses, airline pilots, policemen, ministers, business executives, and others in authority typically dress in these colors.

The world is caught up in fashion. It is a billion-dollar business. The spirit of the world can attach itself to God's people, and they can be consumed with looking good. It is natural for a woman to desire to look beautiful and well pleasing. Women should adorn themselves as beautifully as they can, but it should not consume them. We must get our closet in order and then get on with the business of life. Here is where discipline, planning, good shopping, and adequate organization come into focus.

God wants His people to dress modestly and with "shamefacedness" (propriety), drawing attention to Him rather than putting on the ornaments of the world that distract from His holiness.

Exodus tells about the forming of the golden calf by Aaron, using gold jewelry brought from Egypt, while Moses was on the mountaintop with God. What was God's response? "And the LORD said unto Moses, Go, get thee down; for thy people, which thou broughtest out of the land of Egypt, have corrupted themselves: they have turned aside quickly out of the way which I commanded them: they have made them a molten calf, and have worshipped it, and have sacrificed thereunto, and said, These be thy gods, O Israel, which have brought thee up out of the land of Egypt" (Exodus 32:7-8).

God was so angry that He told Moses, "Now therefore let me alone, that my wrath may wax hot against them, and that I may consume them: and I will make of thee a great nation" (Exodus 32:10).

The jewelry that they had brought up from Egypt had become their death sentence. If they had left the ornaments of the heathen in Egypt, this temptation never would have been fulfilled. Thankfully, Moses interceded. The Lord's anger was abated and He did not destroy them.

But let us notice what happened when Moses talked to the people about their sin and told them how God was going to punish them. "And when the people heard these evil tidings, they mourned: and no man did put on him his ornaments. For the LORD had said unto Moses, Say unto the children of Israel, Ye are a stiffnecked people: I will come up into the midst of thee in a moment, and consume thee: therefore now put off thy ornaments from thee, that I may know what to do unto thee. And the children of Israel stripped themselves of their ornaments by the mount of Horeb" (Exodus 33:4-6).

What happened to the jewelry? God gave instructions to Moses to build a Tabernacle, and Moses asked the people to bring an offering to build it. "And they came, both men and women, as many as were willing hearted, and brought bracelets, and earrings, and rings, and tablets, all jewels of gold: and every man that offered offered an offering of gold unto the LORD" (Exodus 35:22).

God allowed the Israelites to bring the gold of Egypt with them out of their land of bondage, not to heap it on themselves and corrupt their worship, but to give it to Him, so that the place of worship might be adorned with gold, which signified His glory and majesty.

I Timothy 2:9-10 states about the ornaments of the world: "In like manner also, that women adorn themselves in modest apparel, with shamefacedness and sobriety; not with broided hair, or gold, or pearls, or costly array; but (which becometh women professing godliness) with good works."

Here are several other translations of phrases in these verses:

- "With modesty and self-restraint" (*The New Testament of Our Lord and Saviour Jesus Christ,* John Broadus et al.)
- "Modestly and discreetly" (*The New Testament: A New Translation,* Olaf M. Norlie)
- "Modest and refined" (*The New Testament according to the Eastern Texts,* George M. Lamsa)
- "Adorning themselves with reverence and self-restraint" (*The Centenary Translation: The New Testament in Modern English,* Helen Bartlett Montgomery)
- "And their demeanor should be modest and serious" (*The New Testament in Modern English,* J. B. Phillips)
- "And not with wreaths or gold ornaments for the hair" (*The Twentieth Century New Testament)*
- "Not with plaitings and ornamentation of gold" (*The Emphasized New Testament: A New Translation,* J. B. Rotherham)

- "But, as is appropriate for women who profess to be religious" (*The New Testament: An American Translation,* Edgar J. Goodspeed).

I Peter 3:3-5 speaks about the ornaments that a Christian woman should be adorned with: "Whose adorning let it not be that outward adorning of plaiting the hair, and of wearing of gold, or of putting on of apparel; but let it be the hidden man of the heart, in that which is not corruptible, even the ornament of a meek and quiet spirit, which is in the sight of God of great price. For after this manner in the old time the holy women also, who trusted in God, adorned themselves, being in subjection unto their own husbands."

Some have said, "Well, Peter didn't really mean that you couldn't adorn the hair and wear gold, because then you wouldn't have to wear any clothes." There is a common rule among theologians, namely, that we should not try to build a doctrine on one verse of Scripture. Every interpretation must be substantiated by considering all related passages of Scripture. I Peter echoes I Timothy when it talks about putting on of apparel. Obviously I Peter does not forbid the wearing of all apparel but it refers to costly apparel. When we take I Timothy and I Peter together the meaning becomes clearer. Our adorning should not be the outward adorning of plaiting the hair with gold, or the wearing of gold, or the putting on of costly apparel.

An *ornament* is something that is added to decorate,

embellish, or adorn; that which adds grace or beauty. In music it means an embellishing note or notes not belonging to the essential harmony or melody, and it is either indicated by the composer or introduced by the performer for purely decorative effect.

The only piece of jewelry that would not be a decoration would be a wedding band, which signifies the sacred vows of a marriage union. This piece of jewelry has been a controversial subject for as long as I can remember. The general rule of thumb on this matter is to follow the teaching of your pastor. He is the one who watches for your soul and will give an account to God for your behavior.

Let us examine more closely the words in I Timothy 2:9-10, particularly the words *modest*, *shamefacedness*, and *sobriety*. The word *sobriety* is from the Greek word *sophrosune*. It means "prudence, moderation." Women are to clothe themselves in modest apparel with moderation.

> The English word "moderation" is used in Philippians 4:5: "Let your moderation be known unto all men." Here the Greek word gives the idea of gentleness and patience, rather than an aggressive attitude. Why ought we to let our moderation be known to all? Because "the Lord is at hand," or "nigh." The nearness of the Lord Jesus pressures us to keep important things important, and unimportant things in their place. Jesus is

> coming back for His redeemed. When we face Him, we'll be ashamed if we have let a temporal thing like clothing control our lives."[19]

Once more let us come back to what the Jewish women have learned about the wearing of pants. In the Old Testament there were three areas of law: civil, moral, and ceremonial. The moral laws were not abolished at Calvary. One of those laws was found in Deuteronomy 22:5: "The woman shall not wear that which pertaineth unto a man, neither shall a man put on a woman's garment: for all that do so are abomination unto the LORD thy God."

Does verse 5 fall into the category of the ceremonial or moral law? We have an important clue. It says, "All that do so are abomination unto the LORD." God never used this phrase when speaking about the ceremonial law.

> The essence of ceremonial law was the Jews would make certain things unclean to themselves. They were to make some things "an abomination *to you*." Deuteronomy 14 and Leviticus 11 both list a number of such things. "He is unclean *to you*" (Lev. 11:7). "All fowls that creep, going upon all four, shall be an abomination *unto you*" (Lev. 11:20). All such prohibitions made to Jews in the Old Testament are canceled in the New Testament. But every single time the phrase "an abomination *to me,*" when God is speaking, or

> "an abomination *to God*" is used, the Scripture there is forbidding a gross moral sin, something inherently and obviously wrong, and equally condemned in the New Testament. Idolatry is an abomination to God (Deut. 7:25), witchcraft (Deut. 18:10-12), murder and lying (Prov. 6:16-19; 11:20; 12:22). These are an abomination to God. Therefore, when God says it is an abomination to Him when a woman wears a man's clothes, we must conclude this is a moral command, not ceremonial. This sin is in the same class with the gross sins of idolatry, adultery, and murder.[20]

As we have seen, I Timothy 2:9 states for women to wear modest apparel. The word *apparel* is from the Greek word *katastole*, and Young's *Analytical Concordance* translates it "long robe." A robe is not pants. The only pants mentioned in the Bible is when the priests were commanded to wear "breeches" to cover the loins and thighs when they walked up the steps to minister at the altar. (See Exodus 28:42.)

The subject of women's dress and modesty was preached about by the apostles, the leaders of the early church, because it was important. One of those reasons is that God wants to keep the separation of the sexes He created in the beginning.

In the New Testament, Paul, who was moved on by the Holy Ghost, explained that the sins and immorality of people would lead to further sins of homosexuality and lesbianism: "Because that, when they knew God, they glorified him not as God, neither were thankful; but became vain in their imaginations, and their foolish heart was darkened. . . . Wherefore God also gave them up to uncleanness through the lusts of their own hearts, to dishonour their own bodies between themselves: who changed the truth of God into a lie, and worshipped and served the creature more than the Creator, who is blessed for ever. Amen. For this cause God gave them up unto vile affections: for even their women did change the natural use into that which is against nature: and likewise also the men, leaving the natural use of the woman, burned in their lust one toward another; men with men working that which is unseemly, and receiving in themselves that recompense of their error which was meet. And even as they did not like to retain God in their knowledge, God gave them over to a reprobate mind, to do those things which are not convenient" (Romans 1:21, 24-28).

These sinners received recompense for their own ways. They awarded themselves judgment. They chose not to listen to God's Word, so He gave them up to further sin. When He let go of them, they slipped into the abyss of filth and became demoralized. They became vain, which means to manifest undue or excessive pride in one's appearance or attainments and to desire admiration of oneself. Vanity always brings emptiness. Because they became vain, it changed them and their attitude towards God, which in turn brought about an attitude change in God toward them.

God is concerned about keeping the sexes distinct. In *Zondervan's Pictorial Dictionary,* the article on ancient Hebrew women's dress explains:

> A few articles of female clothing carried somewhat the same name and basic pattern, yet there was always sufficient difference in embossing, embroidery, and needlework so that in appearance the line of demarcation between men and women could be readily detected.

God made a difference between men and women and expected them to stay that way. The story is told about a little girl who always wore a dress to school. Some of the other children would tease her because she did not wear pants like the other girls. One day the teacher had them all draw stick figures of men and women. Most of the children put pants on the man and a skirt on the woman. The little girl saw the drawings and said, "That's why I wear skirts. I'm a girl."

What we wear is important. It is all about making a statement as to whom you belong. A prostitute is known by her attire, as Proverbs 7:10 demonstrates: "And, behold, there met him a woman with the attire of an harlot, and subtil of heart." An army officer is identified by his uniform. Why do people get skittish when God talks to them about what they can wear and what they cannot?

Most businesses have their dress codes. Many schools have their dress codes. The army and marines have dress codes. Why should not God, who is much more important than the earthly organizations?

Dress is much more important than affecting our appearance; it helps shape our character. It is well known that people act differently according to what they have on. Clothes not only help shape a person's actions and attitudes, they provide identification and communicate what we are trying to say with our lives.

The word *shamefacedness* mentioned in I Timothy 2:9 is from the Greek word *aidos.* It means "modesty or reverence."

> Thayer's *Greek Lexicon* says *aidos* is objective in its reference, having regard to others. This seems to intimate a woman will dress herself with an awareness of how it will affect others. Trench, another Greek scholar, says this sense of shame, or modesty, precedes and prevents a shameful act. It will restrain a good man from an unworthy act. So a woman ought to dress with *shamefacedness*, sensing a responsibility for her effect on others.[21]

Following are comments on I Timothy 2:9 taken from *The Full Life Study Bible*:

> It is God's will that Christian women be com-

> mitted to dressing modestly and discreetly. (1) The word "shamefacedness" (Gk. *aidos*) implies a certain shame in exposing the body. It involves a refusal to dress in such a way as to draw attention to the body and to pass the boundaries of proper reserve. The source of modesty is in a person's heart or inner character. In other words modesty is the outward manifestation of an inward chastity or purity.
>
> (2) Dressing in an immodest manner that may excite impure desires in others is as wrong as the immoral desire it provokes. No activity or condition justifies the wearing of immodest apparel that exposes the body in such a way as to cause immoral desire or lust in someone else (cf. Gal. 5:13: Eph. 4:27; Tit. 2:11-12; see Mat. 5:28, note).
>
> (3) It is a sad commentary on any church when the Biblical standard for modest dress is ignored and the world's customs are passively adopted. In a day of sexual permissiveness the church should act and dress differently from a corrupt society that casts aside and ridicules the Holy Spirit's desire for modesty and purity.

A woman or girl is responsible to cover herself well. It is not just the length of the skirt, but a neckline should not be too deep, a sweater or top too tight, a fabric too clinging. Not only is the purpose of a woman's dress to cover her well, but modestly. The lines should cover her secret parts in a modest manner. Some of the fashion designers of this generation have even tried to corrupt the wearing of skirts by making them in such a way as to emphasize a woman's figure. Some people would say that pants are more modest than skirts. This is true in some cases, because some fashion designers have designed skirts for the sole purpose of attracting the eyes of an individual to a woman's legs, rear, and thighs. It is to excite immorality. These type of skirts are condemned by the Scripture, and God hates what excites sin.

The bottom line is that God says it is an abomination for a woman to wear men's apparel, but in choosing skirts the guideline is modesty not sexiness. If Satan cannot get a woman to wear pants, he will still try to corrupt what God has tried to make holy.

At a conference recently, several girls who walked by made me feel embarrassment. Their skirts were so tight that everything showed, even their underwear. This is not modesty! I thought, Don't these girls read the Bible? Don't they have a mirror?

Let us notice what the Proverbs 31 woman did concerning her clothing. She is the ideal woman for all women to strive to be like. "She maketh herself coverings of tapestry; her clothing is silk and purple." (Proverbs 31:22). This description signifies quality, grace, and beauty. It was her clothing with which she covered herself well, not ornaments. She covered herself. Here are definitions of *cover*:

1. To place or spread something over.
    a. To place a covering over something, to protect it or to preserve its contents.
    b. To envelop; to clothe, as with a mantle or cloak.
    c. To overwhelm; to spread over.

2. To conceal, screen or shield.
    a. To shelter, as from evil or danger; to protect; to defend.
    b. To hide from sight; to conceal; to cloak; to shield.

How could a woman spread pants over the body? How could pants become a cloak? How could a woman hide or conceal her secret parts with a pair of pants? How can a woman's honor be preserved when she lets her bosom hang out and she accentuates her hips?

Why is God concerned with women dressing in a godly, modest fashion? It makes a statement to the world, telling everyone to whom we belong. It helps us act in a certain way. It causes less temptation to sin. It is the commandment of the Scripture, and its roots are found in obedience to God. It helps keep us in alignment with God's morality.

Do you want to be beautiful? You can, but do it God's way. Psalm 90:17 says, "Let the beauty of the LORD our God be upon us."

Make up your mind that the influence of ungodly

fashion designers and Hollywood's fashions will not dictate to you. You are in the world, but not of the world, so dress according to the fashions of heaven, a place where you are going to live forever. It is a place of purity. Remember while you are on earth that it is just a dressing room for eternity. If you need to change, I dare you to do so. Seek to bring God's purity back into your home, community, city, and church. Dress to please God, and you will be making a difference in the moral decay of our nation.

The Witness of the Spirit

What is a witness? A witness is one who can no longer be himself! *He finds himself inhabited by the Holy Spirit of God, the indwelling Spirit of Christ. All he does at work, at home, at play bears the evidence of that fact. That is "witness." Witness is more than living according to a certain pattern; it is simply the very person of God within me, revealing something of Himself in all that I am and in all that I do, in every situation.*

—Ralph W. Neighbour, Jr.

CHAPTER EIGHT

Holy in Body

God's desire is that His glory would rest upon us. Our body is to let the glory of the Lord shine through us!

I Corinthians 6:19-20 clearly states that a Christian's body is the temple of God. "What? know ye not that your body is the temple of the Holy Ghost which is in you, which ye have of God, and ye are not your own? For ye are bought with a price: therefore glorify God in your body, and in your spirit, which are God's."

We do not own our own bodies; God owns them! Immediately before the preceding passage, the Bible says, "Flee fornication. Every sin that a man doeth is without the body: but he that committeth fornication sinneth against his own body" (I Corinthians 6:18).

Fornication is not holy. It is filthy to God. Fornication is not only a sin against God, but it also hurts the persons who partake in this sin.

I Thessalonians 4:3-4 says that a person should have control over his body and not give in to the weakness of the flesh: "For this is the will of God, even your sanctification, that ye should abstain from fornication: that every one of you should know how to possess his vessel in sanctification and honour."

I Corinthians 10 lists five sins that Moses had to deal with while leading the Israelites through the wilderness. They are the same sins that men and women deal with today. They are as follows:

1. Lust
2. Idolatry
3. Fornication
4. Tempting Christ
5. Murmuring

"Now these things were our examples, to the intent we should not lust after evil things, as they also lusted. Neither be ye idolaters, as were some of them; as it is written, The people sat down to eat and drink, and rose up to play. Neither let us commit fornication, as some of them committed, and fell in one day three and twenty thousand. Neither let us tempt Christ, as some of them also tempted, and were destroyed of serpents. Neither murmur ye, as some of them also murmured, and were destroyed of the destroyer" (I Corinthians 10:6-10).

There needs to be a renewal of old-fashioned respect for the things of God, a reverence for God's Word, and a trembling in His presence.

As Proverbs 9:10 says, "The fear of the LORD is the beginning of wisdom: and the knowledge of the holy is understanding." The important thing is to have the *fear of the Lord*. To fear, respect, or hold God in awe is the beginning of true wisdom.

Profound reverence characterized the ancient copyists of the Scriptures. It is said that when they came to a name for the Deity, they put new pens into their writing instruments, took a bath, and changed clothing.

For months Eric Liddell trained for the purpose of winning the hundred-meter race at the Olympic races of 1924. Many sportswriters predicted that he would win. Then Eric learned the hundred-meter race was scheduled for Sunday. This posed a problem. Eric believed that he could not honor God by running in the contest on the Lord's day. His fans were stunned by his refusal. Some who had praised him now called him a fool. But Eric stood firm.

Suddenly a runner dropped out of the four-hundred-meter race, scheduled on a weekday. Eric offered to fill the slot, even though this race was four times as long as the one for which he had trained. When the race was run, Eric Liddell set a record of 47.6 seconds. He was the winner.

May this book be a wakeup call to those who have lost their respect for God and His Word. Some are playing around with fire, entertaining lustful thoughts, and considering having an affair. There are demonic spirits that are grouped together and that are targeting Christians and even ministers to fall into the trap of sexual sins.

I recently read the story of a young, good-looking girl who was enslaved to almost every vice one could name. She drank heavily, smoked heavily, and took drugs. Her sex life had no restraint. Yet her main aim was to seduce Christian workers and ministers.

Once at a Christian house party her intelligent questions and answers brought her to the attention of the minister leading it. After talking with her, he took her back to the manse to counsel her further. She said that although she wanted to become a Christian she was not able to. The minister tried praying with her, but the girl just could not pray. About to repeat a verse of the Bible by way of comfort, the minister put his hand on her shoulder. Immediately he felt a shock go right through him. Everything went black, and he felt himself sinking into a bottomless pit. A cry of terror escaped from his lips.

On hearing this, some other helpers at the conference rushed into the room, closely followed by his wife. After a few minutes, although it seemed like hours to the minister, he regained consciousness. The girl looked at him and, with an evil expression on her face, asked him,

'Do you know who I am now? I've shot down others already."

The girl later confessed that she had succeeded in seducing a well-known Christian worker. She had led the man on and let him talk to her on theological matters but then had succeeded in getting him to commit adultery with her. She even gave his name. After his experience with this demonically affected girl, the minister was depressed for three weeks.

This is not the time to be dull of mind, but it is time to be alert and aware. It is no time to give up the precious gospel and the hope that is set before each Christian. It is time to rise in new holiness and not succumb to the temptations that Satan is putting before the church.

What this generation needs is old-fashioned godliness. There is too much unbridled passion in every business, even in high places. Titus 2:12 commands Christians to live godly lives: "Teaching us that, denying ungodliness and worldly lusts, we should live soberly, righteously, and godly, in this present world."

Godliness is profitable to a person. I Timothy 4:7-8 states, "But refuse profane and old wives' fables and exercise thyself rather unto godliness. For bodily exercise profiteth little: but godliness is profitable unto all things, having promise of the life that now is, and of that which is to come."

Here are definitions of what it means to be godly:

- Pertaining to, or emanating from God.

- Reverencing God and His laws; obedient to the commands of God.

- Characterized by a devout spirit or mental attitude that leads to frequent prayer or worship.

- Devoted to the things of God, showing fervor and reverence in religious matters.

- Being moral, which is characterized by excellence in what pertains to practice or conduct; that which is right and proper.

- Being noble; conforming to a standard of what is right or good.

- Careful observance of or conformity to the laws of God.

How can someone live in a state of holiness? II Peter 1:3-6 gives the secret: "According as his divine power hath given unto us all things that pertain unto life and godliness, through the knowledge of him that hath called us to glory and virtue: whereby are given unto us exceeding great and precious promises: that by these ye might be partakers of the divine nature, having escaped the corruption that is in the world through lust. And beside this, giving all diligence, add to your faith virtue; and to virtue knowledge; and to knowledge temperance; and to temperance patience; and to patience godliness."

Christians are partakers of God's divine nature. It is His power that gives a person strength to live a holy life.

It is important to guard against the sins of the fleshly body. Galatians 5:16-17 shows that we can have victory over these things if we walk in the Spirit: "This I say then, Walk in the Spirit, and ye shall not fulfil the lust of the flesh. For the flesh lusteth against the Spirit, and the Spirit against the flesh: and these are contrary the one to the other: so that ye cannot do the things that ye would."

Galatians 5:19-21 lists the works of the flesh:

- Adultery: sexual unfaithfulness of a married person.

- Fornication: sexual intercourse on the part of an unmarried person.

- Uncleanness: foul, dirty, filthy, unwholesome behavior.

- Lasciviousness: wantonness, lewdness, lustfulness.

- Idolatry: worship of a physical object; excessive veneration for anything.

- Witchcraft: the practice of witches; sorcery; practice of black magic.

- Hatred: strong aversion coupled with ill will.
- Variance: in a state of dissension; quarrelsomeness.
- Emulations: envious rivalries.
- Wrath: violent anger.
- Strife: violent contention.
- Seditions: insurrections against authority.
- Heresies: religious opinions opposed to the accepted belief that tend to promote schism.
- Envyings: malice; spite; jealousy.
- Murders: destruction of life; putting an end to life.
- Drunkenness: state of being drunk, intoxicated.
- Revellings: disorder; riots.
- And such like.

"They which do such things shall not inherit the kingdom of God" (Galatians 5:21).

A person who commits these sins can be forgiven, sanctified, and made clean, as the following story shows:

> At an open-air Gospel meeting the preacher asked for testimonies. While this was going on, a skeptic was passing by just when the testimony of a saved drunkard was being given. He stopped and listened. The former drunkard was telling how Jesus had wrought a miracle and saved his poor soul.
>
> The skeptic scoffingly made a few remarks to those standing near him. He said "it was nothing more than a dream, religion saving a man in this manner; just a mere dream, and nothing more." No one answered him; but God had His way of dealing with him.
>
> Among the listeners was a little girl about ten years old. She had known the misery of a drunkard's home. She heard the remark of the skeptic and, going up to him, she said: "Please, sir, if it is only a dream, please don't wake him—that is my daddy!"[22]

All these sins can be forgiven, as I Corinthians 6:9-11 demonstrates: "Know ye not that the unrighteous shall not inherit the kingdom of God? Be not deceived: neither fornicators, nor idolaters, nor adulterers, nor effeminate, nor abusers of themselves with mankind, nor thieves, nor covetous, nor drunkards, nor revilers, nor extortioners, shall inherit the kingdom of God. And such were some of you: but ye are washed, but ye are sanctified, but ye are justified in the name of the Lord Jesus, and by the Spirit of our God."

Not only does this passage identify fornication and adultery as sins, but it also says the "effeminate" cannot inherit the kingdom of God. It is an abomination to God to live the homosexual lifestyle. Pornography can feed this sin and lead to other horrible sins. I received an e-mail from a lady who had been delivered from the debilitating lifestyle of lesbianism, and she told me that her problem started with pornography on the Internet.

People are not born as homosexuals, although the sinful tendencies and weaknesses of parents and grandparents can be handed down from generation to generation, through heredity and environment. But of course, Christ came to set people free from those sins and break the generational cycle of sin!

Like adultery and fornication, the homosexual lifestyle is a hideous sin born out of the filth of hell. While God loves all sinners, including those who commit sexual sins, the following verses portray God's disgust with the sin of homosexual behavior.

"Thou shalt not lie with mankind, as with womankind: it is abomination" (Leviticus 18:22).

"If a man also lie with mankind, as he lieth with a woman, both of them have committed an abomination: they shall surely be put to death" (Leviticus 20:13).

The sins of homosexuality and lesbianism (a lesbian

is a homosexual woman) do not have the approval of God! They are not an alternate lifestyle with God! This sin is a cursed thing and brings only destruction, as shown in the story of Sodom and Gomorrah.

God said the sin was very grievous to Him (Genesis 18:20). The sad story is narrated in Genesis 19. Two angels came to Sodom in the evening time. Lot, who was sitting at the gate of Sodom, saw them and went to meet them, bowing himself to the ground. Lot asked them to stay at his house for the night, but they declined, saying they would stay in the street all night.

Lot pressed them to come home with him, so they did. He prepared a feast for them and they ate. Before they went to bed, however, the men of Sodom, both young and old, crowded around the house, and called to Lot, "Where are the men which came in to thee this night? bring them out unto us, that we may know them" (Genesis 19:5). (In this passage the word *know* is a euphemism for sexual intercourse.)

Lot went outside and had the audacity to offer the men his two daughters in place of the angels, but the filthy minds of the men refused even this. The next day God sent destruction upon the wicked city that was characterized by homosexuality. "Then the LORD rained upon Sodom and upon Gomorrah brimstone and fire from the LORD out of heaven" (Genesis 19:24).

Abraham got up early in the morning. "And he looked toward Sodom and Gomorrah, and toward all the land of the plain, and beheld, and, lo, the smoke of the country went up as the smoke of a furnace" (Genesis 19:28).

As low as humans can descend, God is able to bring them back to holiness. The following legend, told by J. A. Clarke, illustrates this truth:

> When God was about to create man, says a Jewish legend, He took into His counsel the angels that stood about His throne. "Create him not," said the angel of Justice, "for if Thou dost he will commit all kinds of wickedness against his fellow men; he will be hard and cruel and dishonest and unrighteous."
>
> "Create him not," said the angel of Truth, "for he will be false and deceitful to his brother-man, and even to Thee."
>
> "Create him not," said the angel of Holiness. "He will follow that which is impure in Thy sight and dishonor Thee to thy face."
>
> Then stepped forward the angel of Mercy (God's best beloved) and said: "Create him, our Heavenly Father, for when he sins and turns from the path of right and truth and holiness I will take him tenderly by the hand, and speak loving words to him, and then lead him back to Thee."[23]

Holy Hair

God gave woman her hair for her glory.
He made it beautiful, shiny, and long.
He created it for Himself—who is most holy,
And when His angels see it, they burst into song.

A woman's hair that bounces when she walks
Announces to the world His infinite grace.
Given to women so that she could have power,
God's love is seen shining through her hair and face.

A woman who has given her whole self to God
Is set apart for a depraved world to see.
They may not understand, but silently they applaud
The glory and discipline of her silent humility!

—Joy Haney

CHAPTER NINE

HOLY HAIR

The following comments about hair are taken from an article in Family Circle *several years ago entitled "Head Lines: What Your Hair Says about You."*

> **Hair**: It's a four-letter word that can spell disaster or delight. If it looks good, we feel good. But if it doesn't, even the most confident among us turn indecisive and insecure. Indeed, how you feel about your hair can affect your self-esteem, your sexuality, even your day-to-day actions. Find out about this ultimate love/hate relationship, and while you're at it, brush up on some hair advice from a styling pro.

Self-Esteem

Some women [of the world] won't leave the house unless their makeup is perfect, while others couldn't care less. But almost everyone will stop to fuss with her hair. The reason? "Your hair is intimately tied up with your self-image," states Dr. Judith Kuriansky, clinical psychologist and call-in host of a WABC-radio advice show.

"It's the first thing people notice about you, so you rely on it to make an impression. If it looks right, everything else falls into place, and you feel great."

Dr. William Cheshier, a practicing psychologist in Chicago and consultant to Alberto Culver, takes the hair-image connection one step further: "The way you perceive your hair affects the way people perceive you. For example, if a woman *thinks* her hairstyle is elegant, she acts that way. The rest of the world might not see the style as elegant, but they'll respond to her idea of herself." He sums it up by explaining that "hair is a lot like sex. It's a reflection of who and what you are."

Sexuality

"Hair is very erotic . . . and the way you wear it is an erotic tool for attracting the opposite sex," states Dr. Ernest Dichter, the psychologist and cultural anthropologist who pioneered motivational research. "Part of the reason long hair is regarded as sexy is that it's so 'caressable': Men can run their fingers through it or bury their face in it. And letting your hair loose is like the phrase 'letting your hair down'—it denotes freedom."

Change

Why do so many run to the hairdresser when something traumatic happens in their lives? According to Dr. Cheshier, when a woman goes through an emotional upheaval, she tends to want to remove all trappings of the past . . . and the easiest way to do that is with a haircut. "Changing your hairstyle," adds Dr. Dichter, "is a renewal, a fresh start." Dr. Kuriansky sums it up this way: "Remember, hair is a big impression maker. So, when you change your hair, you're telling the world you've changed yourself."

At the bottom of the page were these words: "'Hair is an outward symbol of the inner personality.' Dr. Ernest Dichter, psychologist."

At the top left-hand side of the page were these words: "Psychologists talk about the power of hair over your emotions and how hair can reveal your inner self."

A young woman who came to our church was filled with the Holy Ghost. Without anyone saying anything to her, she threw away all her makeup and began to let her butch haircut grow out. These were her words to me about her hair: "I have been hurt by several men in my life, and every time I get hurt, I go to the hairdresser and have them whack my hair off. Psychologically, I want to be unattractive to the men who hurt me. I don't want them to be able to run their fingers through my hair. My emotions really do control what I do with my hair."

I was intrigued by her comments and very surprised, but the article from *Family Circle* supports her thinking to a degree. I spoke to another young woman, and she gave me an entirely different answer. I asked her, "Why do women cut or trim their hair?" She replied, "Women cut their hair because they want to feel attractive and to make themselves look attractive. When your life is out of control, you at least have control over your hair. It makes women feel like they are in control."

The two answers were totally different, but they both deal with how women feel. Clearly, emotions are related to what a woman does with her hair.

As I stood in a health store recently, a woman walked in and was greeted by an older gentleman. He said, "You look a little different." She replied, "I've darkened my hair." Then she laughed and said, "It's easier to change my hair than get a divorce."

The women around her laughed and she said, "You know how we women are. The first thing we do when our world goes topsy-turvy is do something to our hair."

When we went out to the car, my daughter asked me what she meant about the statement, "It's easier to change my hair than get a divorce."

I told her that when a woman feels threatened by rejection, or if maybe there is another woman involved, she wants to do something to change or spruce up her image or the way she looks. One of the major areas of change usually involves the hair. Hair is definitely connected to the emotions of a woman.

"Does it matter whether I trim my hair or not?" is the question that many women today ask. It does matter, and to see why let us examine I Corinthians 11.

I Corinthians 11 is called the "hair chapter" in the Bible. But it deals with more than hair. It is about submission, power, obedience, and the oneness of God.

The chapter first describes the divine order of creation. This chapter is about origin and authority. "But I would have you know, that the head of every man is Christ; and the head of the woman is the man; and the head of Christ is God" (I Corinthians 11:3). God *was* from the beginning; He is Alpha and Omega. Next in divine order is the man Christ, whose sacrifice was planned from the foundation of the world as the basis of our salvation. Then God created the man and afterward the woman. Thus God's Word is supreme over all creation.

A woman who recognizes that there is one God, who is Creator of all, and respects His divine order and plan, will leave her hair long and uncut. God then commits Himself to hear and answer her prayers.

Here are comments on I Corinthians 11 from *The Full Life Study Bible*:

Ordinances were instructions relating to doctrine, moral standards, and codes of conduct that Paul delivered to the churches by the authority of Christ. Note that the content and instruction of ch. 11 outlines God's will for His people in such matters as outward dress, modesty, appearance, and proper conduct. To teach that God is concerned only with inner attitudes and not with "externals" departs from God's clear revelation in Scripture. To dress properly and modestly is a Biblical principle of lasting validity.

Paul is concerned about the proper relationship between men and women, and he seeks to uphold that relationship as ordained by God. (1) He maintains that in Christ a perfect spiritual equality exists among men and women as heirs of God's grace, yet it is an equality involving order and subordination with respect to authority. . . . The word "head" seems to express both authority and origination.

(2) Paul bases the husband's headship not on cultural considerations, but on God's creative activity and purpose in creating the women to help the man.

(3) Subordination is not demeaning to one's person, for it does not imply suppression or oppression. Rather it states that the husband must recognize the worth God places upon the woman and that his responsibility involves pro-

tecting and leading her in such a way as to fulfill God's will for her in the home and the church.

I Corinthians 11:6-10 states, "For if the woman be not covered, let her also be shorn: but if it be a shame for a woman to be shorn or shaven, let her be covered. For a man indeed ought not to cover his head, forasmuch as he is the image and glory of God: but the woman is the glory of the man. For the man is not of the woman; but the woman of the man. Neither was the man created for the woman; but the woman for the man. For this cause ought the woman to have power on her head because of the angels."

This passages reveals the following points:

1. It is a shame for a woman to be shorn or shaven.

2. Woman is the glory of the man—she was created for the man to be his glory and helpmate.

3. Her uncut hair is a symbol of her recognition of who God is, her respect for His Word, and her submission to her husband.

4. Since woman was the one to cause the fall in the Garden of Eden, this is her display of obedience rather than disobedience.

The angels watch women to see whether they are in

submission to God's Word—not only the angels in heaven, but the fallen angels watch also. Women are surrounded continually by a great army of spiritual beings who are gazing upon their actions and attitudes.

A woman who is submissive to God and who has a consistent prayer life, has much power in the spirit world. She can take authority over demons and they have to flee. She can speak to cancer and command it to leave. She has authority over the evil one, and as long as she stays in a state of humility and prayer, hell cannot win over her.

She has great power over the enemy! Not only does she have power in her prayer life, but she is a testimony to the world that she respects the sacred Word of God and His deity.

Some people in the modern age feel that the cutting of the hair is not important. But why would God devote a chapter to the hair question if it were not important? The pressure of this society is bearing down upon the church to give in to the worldly system, but it is time for women to stand strong. If we want to have power with God, receive answers to prayer, experience miracles, and walk in authority and influence, then we Christian women should leave the scissors alone. We should not let them come near our heads for any reason.

According to *The American College Dictionary*, the word *shorn* is simply the past participle of *shear*. Therefore, we must look under the word *shear* for the definition. To shear means to cut with shears or other sharp instrument. It means to cut the hair, fleece, or wool. *Strong's Exhaustive Concordance* defines the Greek word *keiro*, which is translated *shorn* in verse six, as simply "to shear."

Our hair is our glory. We do not need to chop it off or let the world's wisdom tell us that split ends need to be trimmed. There are hundreds of products to help split ends.

Do not listen to the modern-day prophets of Baal and the beauty parlor owned by Jezebel. She will tell you to paint your face, cut your hair, and be immodest, but where did she end up? The dogs ate her bones and licked up her polluted, wicked blood, after she fell down from a window in which she was preening herself for all the world to see.

Her wicked heart and vanity were her ruin. The virtuous woman of Proverbs 31 is totally different from Jezebel. God frowned on Jezebel; so should we. We should get our eyes on the ideal woman and become godly women who fear the Lord and walk in the beauty of holiness.

Verse 15 states: "But if a woman have long hair, it is a glory to her: for her hair is given her for a covering."

According to *The New Schaff-Herzog Encyclopedia of Religious Knowledge,* "Women [in Hebrew culture] never cut their hair (cf. Jer. vii, 29), and long hair was their greatest ornament (Cant. iv. 1; cf. I Cor. xi. 15; Cant. vii 5). To cut off a woman's hair and so expose her neck was the greatest contumely [insult] (cf. Jer. vii. 29; I Cor. xi.6)."[24]

The *World Book Encyclopedia* explains the advent of short hair for American ladies: "Short hair styles became popular in the 1920's. Irene Castle, a famous ballroom dancer, started a fashion of *bobbed* (short) hair for women."[25]

John 11:12 provides an example of a woman's long hair: "Now a certain man was sick, named Lazarus, of Bethany, the town of Mary and her sister Martha. (It was that Mary which anointed the Lord with ointment, and wiped his feet with her hair, whose brother Lazarus was sick.)"

What if Mary would have cut her hair off and offered it to the goddess Diana, like the heathen custom of the prostitutes? She never would have been able to dry the feet of Jesus with her long, beautiful hair.

In I Corinthians 11:16, Paul did not write under the inspiration of the Holy Ghost for fifteen verses and then cancel out what he had just written. He started the chapter in verse one by saying, "Be ye followers of me, even as I also am of Christ." It does not make sense for Paul to reject in his own churches the teaching he had set forth so carefully. In fact, that verse states the exact opposite. The New American Standard Bible reads, "But if one is inclined to be contentious, we have no other custom, nor have the churches of God." In other words, if someone wants to fight this doctrine or be contentious about it, there is nothing to argue about, because we have no other doctrine or choice. This is the way; we are to walk in it.

Williams's New Testament translation says, "But if anyone is inclined to be contentious about it, I for my part prescribe no other practice than this, and neither do the churches of God." The verse is simply saying, "We have no custom or manner of contention over this matter. It is beyond contention or argument. It is settled."

Another interesting passage regarding hair is Numbers 5. Here is Elizabeth Rice Handford's description:

> There is a strange and mysterious Scripture in Numbers 5. The chapter tells what a man ought to do if "a spirit of jealousy" seizes him and he fears his wife has been unfaithful to him. He is to bring his wife to the priest. The priest is to make a drink using the dust from the Tabernacle floor. God has ordained the drink to be a terrible curse to the woman if she has been unfaithful to her husband. Her "thigh will rot, and her belly swell." However, if she has been unjustly accused, if she has been a loyal and faithful wife, the poisonous water cannot harm her. God reaches down from Heaven to miraculously protect the pure wife.
>
> But notice what the priest does when the woman is first brought to him. (The meaning is somewhat obscured in the King James, so let me quote it from the NASB.) "The priest shall then have the woman stand before the Lord, and let the hair of the woman's head go loose, and place the grain offering of memorial in her hands,

> which is the grain offering of jealousy and in the hand of the priest is to be the water of bitterness that brings a curse" (Numbers 5:18). The priest first is to "let the hair of the woman's head go loose." What does this mysterious procedure mean, this unpinning of the hair, and letting it fall loose?
>
> Could it not be that, before the test even begins, Heaven and earth can witness whether or not the woman has been living in subjection to her husband, submitting to his protection? And is that witness to be seen in the "loosened" hair, whether it is shorn or not?[26]

These are the last days. The Lord Jesus is coming back soon for His church. This is no time to let down or ponder at the pool of mediocrity. It is time to pull out all the stops and go forward in Jesus' name, walking with grace and the beauty of holiness upon us.

Revival is sweeping the earth in spite of the violence and moral decay. The darker it becomes, the brighter the light of the church will shine. We must make sure there is a distinct difference between the church and the world, for there is no mingling of the two with God.

Do not let the devil steal your glory. Guard it like you would guard a million dollars. You are only on earth a short time, but you will live forever in a pure place, a holy city. You must prepare now for the glory world and not become polluted by the beggarly standards of this world.

The Book of Revelation describes the world in which we hold citizenship: "And I saw a new heaven and a new earth: for the first heaven and the first earth were passed away; and there was no more sea. And I John saw the holy city, new Jerusalem, coming down from God out of heaven, prepared as a bride adorned for her husband. And I heard a great voice out of heaven saying, Behold, the tabernacle of God is with men, and he will dwell with them, and they shall be his people, and God himself shall be with them, and be their God. And God shall wipe away all tears from their eyes; and there shall be no more death, neither sorrow, nor crying, neither shall there be any more pain: for the former things are passed away. . . . And he said unto me, It is done. I am Alpha and Omega, the beginning and the end. I will give unto him that is athirst of the fountain of the water of life freely. He that overcometh shall inherit all things; and I will be his God, and he shall be my son. . . . And he carried me away in the spirit to a great and high mountain, and shewed me that great city, the holy Jerusalem, descending out of heaven from God, having the glory of God: and her light was like unto a stone most precious, even like a jasper stone, clear as crystal; and had a wall great and high, and had twelve gates, and at the gates twelve angels, and names written thereon. . . . And the city had no need of the sun, neither of the moon, to shine in it: for the glory of God did lighten it, and the Lamb is the light thereof. . . . And there shall in no wise enter into it any thing that defileth, neither whatsoever worketh abomination, or maketh a lie: but they which are written in the Lamb's book of life" (Revelation 21:1-4, 6-7, 10-12, 23, 27).

EPILOGUE

It is my fervent prayer that there will be more saints like the white ermine in the following account:

> Such pride does the little white ermine take in his spotless coat, [that] he permits nothing to soil it in the slightest degree. Hunters, well-acquainted with this fact, take unsportsmanlike advantage of him. They do not set traps but daub filth within and around the entrance to his home. As the dogs are loosed and the chase begins, the little animal turns to his one place of refuge. But on seeing the filth, [he] turns to face the yelping dogs, thinking it is better to be stained by blood than sully his white coat![27]

This is the day to pray for courage—courage to do what is pleasing to God, courage to look not to the ways and wisdom of this world but to the age-old wisdom of the Bible. It is the day to demonstrate God's holiness and purity to a world that has gone mad with sexual perversion and moral decay. It is time to dedicate our body, mind, soul, and spirit to Him, who is holy, great, wonderful, majestic, and glorious! May we seek His will as we walk this day, as the following poem says so well.

THY WILL

To know Thy will, Lord of the seeking mind,
To learn Thy way for me, Thy purpose kind,
Thy path to follow and Thy guide find—
    For this I pray.

To do Thy will, Lord of the eager soul,
To bring my restlessness ’neath Thy control,
To give Thee, not a part, but all—the whole—
    For this I pray.

To love Thy will, Lord of the ardent heart,
To bid all selfishness, all sloth depart,
To share with gladness all Thou dost and art—
    For this I pray.

—Alice M. Kyle

NOTES

Chapter 1

[1] J. S. Exell, *The Preacher's Complete Homiletical Commentary on the Old Testament,* (New York: Funk & Wagnall 1892), 35.

[2] Matthew Henry, *Commentary on the Whole Bible* (New York: Fleming H. Revell), 281.

[3] James Hastings, *A Dictionary of the Bible* (New York: Charles Scribner's Sons, 1909), 397-98, citing Cremer, *Bib. Theol. Lex., s.v.*

[4] Hastings, 400.

[5] Paul Lee Tan (Rockville, MD: Assurance Publishers), no. 2231.

Chapter 2

[6] Joseph S. Johnson, *A Field of Diamonds* (Nashville: Broadman Press, 1974), 114.

[7] Walter B. Knight, *Knight's Treasury of Illustrations* (Grand Rapids: William B. Eerdmans, 1963), 360.

[8] Tan, no. 5273.

[9] Ibid., no. 4141.

Chapter 3

[10] Knight, 443.

[11] Ibid., 359.

[12] Ibid., 362.

[13] Tan, no. 824.

Chapter 5

[14] Johnson, 128.

Chapter 6

[15] Knight, 411.

[16] Ibid., 413.

[17] Clinton T. Howell, *Lines to Live By* (Nashville: Thomas Nelson, 1992), 110.

[18] Knight, 413.

Chapter 7

[19] Elizabeth Rice Handford, *Your Clothes Say It for You* (Murfreesboro, TN: Sword of the Lord Publishers, 1976), 26.

[20] Ibid., 47.

[21] Ibid., 74.

Chapter 8

[22] Tan, no. 4972.

[23] Ibid., no. 1935.

Chapter 9

[24] 5:18.

[25] 50th anniv. ed., 11.

[26] Handford, 68-69.

Epilogue

[27] Tan, no. 4854.

About the Author

Joy Haney is a speaker, recording artist, author of fifty-six books, prayer warrior, and wife of Kenneth Haney, who served as general superintendent of the United Pentecostal Church International from 2001-2009, where she served as first lady. She received a Bachelor of Ministry degree from Central Christian College in 1998. She also served as pastor's wife at Christian Life Center, Stockton, California, for thirty years, as prayer leader of live program at KYCC radio station for eleven years, and as chairperson of the Women's Department at Christian Life College for twelve years. She resides in Stockton, California, and is the mother of five children and grandmother of nine.

OTHER BOOKS

by Joy Haney

Paperback

A Call to Holiness
At the Master's Feet, Volume I
Behold the Nazarite Woman
Blessing of the Prison, The
Carpenter, The
Cuando Ayuneis
Dreamers, The
Elite, The
Gold Tried In the Fire
Great Faith
Great Women, The
Healed In the Name of Jesus
Healing Power of Prayer, The
How to Forgive When It's Hard to Forget
How to Have a Wonderful Marriage
How to Have Radiant Health
How to Receive a Miracle
Keeper's of God's Dream
Kenneth F. Haney: A Man With a Vision
Living in the Miracle Level
Magical Gift of Kindness, The
May I Wash Your Feet
Miracles Happen When Women Pray
Modern Day Abraham
Nothing But the Best: A Call to Excellence
Phillip's Family
Power of Speaking Positive
Pray the Word
Pressed Down But Looking Up
Privileged Woman, The
Put On Your War Coat and Fight
Radiant Woman, The
Seeds For Success
Seven Parchments, The
Those Bloomin' Kids
What Do You Do When You Don't Feel Like Doing What You're Doing?
When Ye Fast
When Ye Give
When Ye Pray
Victor Not A Victim
When God Doesn't Deliver On Time
When Mothers Touch Heaven
Women of the Spirit Bible Studies:
Vol. I: Love God's Way
Vol. II: Faith, Prayer & Spiritual Warfare
Vol. III: All About Trials
Vol. IV: Wisdom, Attitudes & Character
Vol. V: Women of Compassion
Vol. VI: The Power of Praise Vol.
Vol. VII: Joy
Vol. VIII: Fruit of Spirit
Vol. IX: Fasting and Prayer

Hardback

A Woman's Cry for Love
(a full-color gift book of English & Italian Sonnets)
Breaking the Alabaster Box
Diamonds for Dusty Roads
His Angels

Cassettes and CD's

Clean Out the Ashes *(book on tape)*
Pray in the Spirit *(singing tape & CD)*